W9-DII-388

SYRIA

Coleman South & Leslie Jermyn

MARSHALL CAVENDISH BENCHMARK

NEW YORK

PICTURE CREDITS

Cover photo: © K.M. Westermann/Corbis

Alamy: 33 • Heino Banderob/Stockfood: 131 • Bes Stock: 8, 48, 51, 60, 108, 117 • V. & M. Birley/www.tropix.co.uk: 45, 46, 47 • Corbis, Inc.: 1, 6, 28, 30, 44, 49, 68, 78, 98 • Hulton Deutsch: 22, 25 • Eye Ubiquitous/Hutchison Library: 10, 128 • Sylvain Grandadam/Age fotostock: 88, 120 • HBL Network Photo Agency: 4, 5, 24, 54, 81, 97, 106, 114, 121 • D.C. Heath: 14, 15, 38, 115 • Hutchison Library: 3, 27, 29, 41, 42, 57, 59, 71, 76, 82, 84, 119, 125 • Hubertus Kanus/ Superstock: 52 • Horst Klemm/Masterfile: 16 • Bjorn Klingwall: 11, 13, 19, 20, 32, 53, 61, 63, 64, 66, 67, 69, 74, 77, 83, 89, 90, 99, 102, 103, 109, 112, 118, 126, 127, 129 • Life File: 7, 39, 55, 91, 92, 93, 94, 95, 124 • Barbara Lutterback /Stockfood: 130 • Christine Osborne: 21, 35, 37, 40, 43, 65, 87, 105, 110, 111, 113, 116, 123 • Doug Scott/Age fotostock: 36 • Jamie Simson: 9, 12, 17, 58, 62, 72, 75, 79, 96, 104, 107 • World Religions/Bes Stock: 117

PRECEDING PAGE

A Syrian girl in the courtyard of the Omayyad Mosque in Damascus.

Marshall Cavendish Benchmark
99 White Plains Road
Tarrytown, NY 10591
Website: www.marshallcavendish.us

© Times Editions Private Limited 1995
© Marshall Cavendish International (Asia) Private Limited 2006
All rights reserved. First edition 1995. Second edition 2006.
® "Cultures of the World" is a registered trademark of Times Publishing Limited.

Originated and designed by Times Editions
An imprint of Marshall Cavendish International (Asia) Private Limited
A member of Times Publishing Limited

Library of Congress Cataloging-in-Publication Data
South, Coleman, 1948-
   Syria / by Coleman South. – 2nd ed.
     p. cm. – (Cultures of the world)
   Summary: "Provides comprehensive information on the geography, history, governmental structure, economy, cultural diversity, peoples, religion, and culture of Syria" – Provided by publisher.
   Includes bibliographical references and index.
   ISBN 0-7614-2054-1
   1. Syria – Juvenile literature. I. Title. II. Series.
   DS93.S66 2006
   956.91 — dc22   2005023848

Printed in China

7 6 5 4 3 2 1

CONTENTS

An elderly Syrian shepherd.

A geometric animal motif typical of Islamic art.

INTRODUCTION

THERE IS AN OLD SYRIAN EXPRESSION, "Everyone has two homelands, their own and Syria." It captures the diversity of cultures and religions that co-exist in modern Syria as well as the array of civilizations that have occupied the territory throughout its history, including the Sumerians, Babylonians, Egyptians, Canaanites, Persians, Greeks, Romans, Ottoman Turks, French, and Arabs.

There are people in Syria who still speak the language of Jesus Christ; they live with representatives of different branches of Islam, and followers of both Judaism and Eastern and Western Orthodox Christianity. Overlaying this historical depth and cultural diversity are the contemporary problems of a middle-income country struggling to educate its people and negotiate a path in the modern world. Syria entered the new millennium with a new leader and fresh hopes for a prosperous and peaceful future.

GEOGRAPHY

MODERN SYRIA was once part of a larger area that included what are now the countries of Syria, Jordan, Lebanon, the Palestinian territories, and Israel. This land has been called the Levant, Greater Syria, and in Arabic, Bilad al Sham (bi-LAD uh-SHAM). It is still often referred to as the Levant.

Geography, vegetation, and weather in Syria are varied, ranging from mountains to steppes, from lush vegetation to barren land, and from moderate to extreme temperatures. Two-thirds of Syria is desert.

LOCATION AND SIZE

Syria borders Jordan on the south, Lebanon on the west, Israel on the southwest, the Mediterranean Sea on the northwest, Turkey on the north, and Iraq on the east and southeast. It has about 90 miles (145 km) of Mediterranean coastline.

The country is shaped somewhat like a triangle with irregular sides. You can drive between any of its borders in less than one day. Although it covers only about 71,500 square miles (185,180 square km), just slightly larger than North Dakota, Syria's strategic location has increased its historical importance to both Middle Eastern and Western civilizations far out of proportion to its size. It is often called "the crossroads of civilizations."

Syria has one Mediterranean island, called Arwad, just off the coast at Tartus. The island was an independent kingdom called Aradus in the days of the Phoenicians and contains many historical structures as well as a marina. Its inhabitants depend on fishing for their livelihoods.

Above: **Grapes grow in abundance along the coast and in the coastal mountains.**

Opposite: **Poppies cover a field in western Syria.**

The triangle of land northeast of the Euphrates and Al Khabur rivers is called Al-Jazirah (zha-ZEER-a), and is not as dry as the central desert. It gets about 10 inches (25.4 cm) of rainfall annually. Although most of the central and southern desert is half a mile (0.8 km) or more above sea level, Al-Jazirah's altitude is around 1,200 feet (360 km). This area was part of ancient Mesopotamia.

GEOGRAPHIC REGIONS AND CLIMATE

The western band of the country, where most of the people live, is less than 60 miles (100 km) wide and has a Mediterranean climate. The coastal plain is one of the most fertile on the Mediterranean. Temperatures range between 70 and 90°F (21 and 32°C) in summer and 50 and 70°F (10 and 21°C) in winter. It is humid on the coast, with annual rainfall averaging 38 inches (96 cm).

To the east is a range of limestone mountains called the Jabal al-Nusayriya, which is cool in summer, and often snow-covered in winter. Between this range and the next is a drier but still fertile valley called the Ghab Depression, which was filled with marshes until modern times. Farther east is a range of dry mountains. The climate around this eastern range is similar, but with warmer summer temperatures and colder winter temperatures than on the coast.

Clouds over the Syrian desert.

The narrow strip of land along the eastern slopes of the coastal mountains is where the largest cities are, and the climate varies quite a bit from south to north. For example, the average rainfall in Aleppo, in the north, is about 18.5 inches (47 cm) per year, but it is only 9 inches (22.8 cm) in Damascus, farther south. But the rainfall increases again south of Damascus. The temperatures along this strip range from over 100°F (37°C) in summer to below freezing in winter.

The reason for the drier area around Damascus is the Anti-Lebanon Mountains. The western spine of this range is in Lebanon and is higher than the coastal mountains of Syria. The eastern spine is higher yet and turns northeastward at Damascus. They end in the geographic center of Syria, east of Palmyra, and block most rainfall.

The area east of the populated strip, with the exception of some mountainous land along the Turkish border and the irrigated land along the three main rivers, is high steppe and rocky, gravel desert. The Syrian Desert, as it is named, also covers a large part of eastern Jordan, western Iraq, and northern Saudi Arabia.

The desert in south-central Syria is an ancient volcanic area covered by rough lava flows and dotted with cinder cones. Some of this land has been painstakingly cleared of lava rock so it can be used for agriculture.

RIVERS

There are several large rivers. The Euphrates enters from Turkey in the northwest, travels east for a distance, then south again, exiting into Iraq in the southeast. It has two tributaries. The Al Balikh River also starts in Turkey, enters Syria in the north, and flows into the Euphrates in north-central Syria. The Al Khabur begins in the northeast and flows into the Euphrates at Deir-ez-Zor, about 100 miles (160 km) from the Iraqi border.

The Barada is a small river that creates the Al-Ghuta Oasis, where the capital city of Damascus stands. The Barada begins in several mountain springs near Damascus and flows northeastward. Although it nearly dries up in the dry season, it has allowed people to live in Damascus for thousands of years.

The Orontes has its sources in Lebanon and flows northward through the Ghab Depression into Turkey, then empties into the Mediterranean. Dams at Homs and Hama on the Orontes have made western Syria agriculturally productive and provided local industry with hydropower.

LIQUID LIFE, LIQUID POWER

The Euphrates River, at 2,100 miles (3,360 km) long, is the largest river in western Asia. It begins on the Anatolian Plateau in eastern Turkey and joins the Tigris River at Basra in southern Iraq, where the two rivers create vast marshlands. Turkey has 40 percent of the river's length inside its borders, Syria only 15 percent, but this small portion has supported civilization in eastern and northern Syria for thousands of years. Although the river is quite wide (in some places nearly a mile), it is mostly shallow with constantly shifting sandbars, and ships cannot navigate it.

The primary use of the river today is for irrigation, although it also provides some fish. Its second most important use is for the generation of electrical power. Construction of the Tabaqah Dam near Raqqa (*below*) was begun in 1968 after extensive archaeological exploration of the upstream portion that would be flooded by the lake. This is Syria's main source of electricity and its only dam on the Euphrates. The dam creates the largest lake in Syria, Lake Al Asad, which is about 50 miles (80.5 km) long and an average of 5 miles (8 km) wide. It holds about 15.6 million cubic yards (12 million cubic meters) of water.

Water is perhaps the most precious resource in the arid Middle East. Disputes over the use of the Euphrates have plagued Syrian-Turkish relations for years, especially since the Turks built a series of dams to permit irrigation of farmland. Syrian farmers complain that they get less water and that it is of less use because the fertile silt has already been deposited on fields upstream. Less water means power shortages in Syria, too. Under President Bashar Al-Asad, Syria has initiated a new era of cooperation with Turkey and hopes to find a solution to this problem soon.

ISLANDS IN THE DESERT

Some of the things that have made life possible in this part of the world are oases. These are lowland places where natural springs surface and allow plants to grow. The most common plants are date palms, but some oases grow bananas and olives as well. Many of the palm trees are centuries old.

There are always small settlements around the water sources, some of them thousands of years old. In the past, these settlements served as caravansaries—resting places for camel caravans.

The spring water is channeled by small canals through plots of land that are often surrounded by ancient adobe walls 6 to 8 feet (2 to 2.5 m) high. These canals may have been the world's first irrigation systems.

The biggest and best known oasis is the one at Tadmor, near the ruins of Palmyra. This oasis was the source of life for the ancient Roman city.

Lush foliage at the oasis at Palmyra.

LAKES

Syria has only two natural lakes; the others were created by dams built for irrigation and electrical power. The biggest of the natural lakes is Arram, which fills the crater of an extinct volcano in the Golan Heights. The other natural lake is Mzerib, northeast of Daraa, which is on the border with Jordan.

The largest artificial lake is Al Asad, created by the Tabaqah Dam. The second largest lake is Qattina, southwest of Homs. This is the main source of the Orontes River, and although it used to be rich with fish, it is now badly contaminated. Another lake, about one-third the size of Qattina, is Al Rastan, formed by a dam on the Orontes River about 12 miles (20 km) north of Homs. About 9 miles (15 km) north of Hama is Lake Karma, another source of water for the Orontes. Lake Baloran, in the mountains northeast of Latakia, was created by a dam on the river of the same name. And finally, Lake Karn is a tiny lake in the mountains west of Damascus, formed by a dam on the Barada River.

CITIES

About half of Syria's population live in cities. Syria's cities have many modern elements side-by-side older neighborhoods. Some have narrow, winding streets, and many buildings have not changed in hundreds of years.

Damascus is one of the oldest continuously inhabited cities in the world. Old Damascus lies on the southern bank of the Barada River. One of its most famous landmarks is the Omayyad Mosque, which was constructed in A.D. 705. Modern Damascus extends north of the Barada. It has wide avenues, large apartment buildings, and tall office complexes. The University of Damascus sits on the outskirts.

Aleppo is also an ancient city, with the earliest settlements dating from about 7,000 years ago. A large 12th-century Arab fort dominates the older part of the city. Modern Aleppo is a commercial and industrial center.

Homs, a heavy industry center, and Latakia, the country's main port on the Mediterranean, were both established by the Greeks around 300 B.C.

Damascus is also the commercial capital of Syria.

Deir-ez-Zor is the center of oil exploration. It is located on the Euphrates River in the southeast, about 60 miles (100 km) from Iraq.

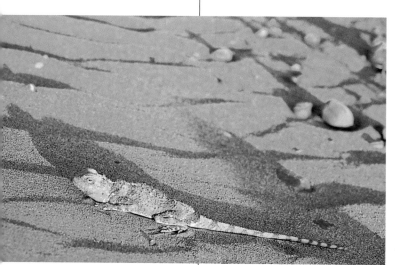

Lizards are common in the desert. Here an *Agama Ruderata* basks in the sun in the Syrian Desert.

FLORA AND FAUNA

Along the coast and in the coastal mountains, pine, olive, and fruit trees, and grapevines are abundant. The cities east of the coastal range have green belts around them where most of their fruit and vegetables have traditionally been grown. This is changing, though, with population growth, and the bigger cities now import most of their produce from rural areas farther away. In and around Damascus, Homs, Hama, and Aleppo, there are olive, eucalyptus, pine, locust, maple, fig, palm, and citrus trees and also many grapevines. Poplars and cottonwoods grow along the rivers on the eastern side of the coastal mountains, and of course, palm trees grow in desert oases and on the edges of the desert. In the cities, jasmine, bougainvillea, orange blossoms, and other flowers provide splashes of color and sweet scents during spring and summer.

No official statistics exist about what animals still roam the deserts and mountains and which ones are endangered or extinct. Scorpions, lizards, and snakes are common in the deserts. Less than a century ago, gazelles, lions, eagles, buzzards, jackals, red foxes, desert hares, and wolves were also common. In medieval times Arab princes used to fight the lions as part of their coming-of-age ritual. They also staged large hunting expeditions for desert creatures.

Sadly, it seems that most larger wildlife in Syria is already gone or on the way to disappearing. The few that remain—gazelles and foxes, for example—are still hunted for sport.

There are several reasons for the disappearance of the wildlife. One is human population growth and its encroachment into all fertile areas of the country. Another is the use of DDT and other poisons that are banned in most Western countries. Yet another is the wild dogs in the desert, kept by Bedouins to protect their sheep. These fierce animals often run in packs and will even attack people. Fragile desert ecosystems are easily disrupted by such human activity and by the introduction of non-native species.

Another reason may be climate change. Over the past few centuries a lot of land that used to be fertile has become desert. In the central desert, for example, there are ruins of Arab palaces once used as hunting lodges. To build and use such permanent structures required regular supplies of food, water, and fuel, none of which is available there now.

The Syrian Desert is different from most deserts in the United States. There is little vegetation other than sparse clumps of short grass in the late winter and early spring and the greenery in a few oases. The grass of the desert and steppes, however, supports Bedouin sheep and goats as it has for millennia.

Gagea reticulata blooms in a Syrian Desert.

15

HISTORY

SYRIA HAS A RICH and culturally diverse history. The coast and the Euphrates River area have remnants of empires and civilizations from as far back as 7,000 years. There are structures still in use today that were built by the Romans, the Arabs, the Ottomans, and the French.

ANCIENT HISTORY

The earliest prehistoric remains of people found in Syria are from the Middle Paleolithic period. Fertility goddess statues and flint and obsidian tools of early peoples have been found in Ugarit, on the Syrian coast.

A thousand years later, settlers began using primitive soft pottery. Then, 4,000 to 5,000 years ago, ceramics in elegant shapes, painted with geometric designs, began to appear. The technology of the pottery slowly improved, and during the first millennium B.C. copper work appeared.

Until around the eighth century B.C., Syria had two mostly separate histories: eastern and western. West of the coastal mountains, the Phoenicians and Aramaeans flourished; in the eastern part of what is now Syria, the Sumerians and the Babylonians built their civilizations.

Left: **An archaeological dig in the Euphrates area of northern Syria. Pottery from early settlers has been found all across northern Syria.**

Opposite: **The Roman theater at Busra. The Romans left many impressive ruins that are still visible today.**

17

WESTERN HISTORY

Around 2000 B.C. the Canaanites moved onto the coastal plain and the seaward side of the coastal mountains in what is now Israel, Lebanon, and Syria. These people were called Phoenicians by the Greeks. This name referred to all the peoples of the area, although none of them called themselves by that name.

The Phoenicians were the first great seafarers, establishing colonies and trading with people all around the Aegean Sea. It was during their time that the already ancient settlement at Ugarit was given its name. They developed and improved iron tools, and had the first royalty that wore purple robes. The purple dye came from a mollusk unique to the Mediterranean shores of Syria. The first known kings were Niqmadou and Yaqaroum. During the 15th century B.C., the Egyptians invaded and conquered parts of Syria but left the Canaanite kingdom intact; the two groups were friendly.

The earliest known alphabetic writing dates from the reign of Niqmadou II (circa 1360–30 B.C.). The writing, in alphabetic cuneiform on tablets, tells much about the customs and institutions of the coastal people. The tablets show that the Canaanite kingdom included a large part of what is now northwestern Syria. They speak of extensive diplomatic activity to safeguard the kingdom from the advance of both the Egyptians on the south and the Hittites on the north.

Thereafter trade, war, and political intrigue became increasingly common among the peoples at this end of the Mediterranean, and Ugarit was finally destroyed around the end of the 13th century B.C. The city never rose again, but during the fifth and fourth centuries B.C., Greek fishermen built some dwellings there, atop a hill that covered thousands of years of buried history, and named the place Leukos Limen.

LANGUAGE AT UGARIT

The development of written language may be the most significant aspect of Syrian history. There were two original types of writing: the hieroglyphic style of Egypt and the alphabetic cuneiform style discovered at Ugarit and in ancient Sumer. Cuneiform was the simplest, consisting of only 30 shapes, one for each letter. The Phoenician alphabet was later used as the basis for Greek, which in turn was the basis for most Western alphabets. Arabic also has its roots in Ugaritic.

The language represented by cuneiform characters—called Ugaritic (*as shown in the picture*)—was one of several languages used in Ugarit. It was spoken by most of the city's population and was used in poems and myths. Babylonian, the international language of the time, was used in diplomatic correspondence and judicial documents. Most of the texts found are in these two languages—Ugaritic and Babylonian—but others have been found in Hurrian (a non-Semitic language of eastern Asia Minor), Cypro-Minoan, Hittite, and Sumerian cuneiform, and Egyptian and Hittite hieroglyphics.

ARAMAEANS Around the end of the 13th century B.C., another Semitic people, known as the Aramaeans, settled east of the coastal mountains. Their kingdom became known as Aram and eventually covered a large part of what is now Syria.

From their capital in Damascus, the Aramaeans developed extensive overland trade with southern Arabia and Persia. They converted the Phoenician alphabet for use with their own language, Aramaic, which became the official language of Syria.

Around 1030 B.C., the Aramaean tribes joined together to attack the Israelites, who were led by King David, but were defeated in three campaigns. The Aramaeans and the Israelites continued to struggle for domination of the area until the eighth century B.C.

Aram prospered for hundreds of years before being destroyed by the Assyrians in 732 B.C.

Aramaic, which is the language Christ spoke, is still spoken today in and around Maalula, a village north of Damascus, and is used in the liturgy of the Syrian Orthodox Church.

EASTERN HISTORY

Around 3000 B.C., the ancient Sumerians (of what is now southern Iraq) spread northeastward into what is now eastern Syria and northern Iraq, eventually occupying most of the land between and around the Euphrates and Tigris rivers. The area is often referred to as Mesopotamia, the Fertile Crescent, and Babylonia. The people became known as Babylonians. Mari, an archaeological site on the Euphrates River near the Iraqi border, has turned up evidence of settlers as far back as the second century B.C. In 1933 the remains of a 300-room palace were uncovered here—one of the biggest palaces ever discovered!

At the same time the Babylonians were developing and expanding, the civilization of the Assyrians was developing on the northern Tigris River. The Assyrians, from whom Syria got its name, were as well known for their military conquests and brutality as the Babylonians were for their accomplishments in science, the arts, and religion.

In 2300 B.C., a group of Semitic people under a leader known as Sargon conquered Babylonia and established the kingdom of Akkad. Not long after, this kingdom fell to Guti tribes from the Zagros Mountains between modern Turkey and Iran. In the 19th century B.C., Amorites, descendants of the Canaanites, conquered the region. The Assyrians took over all of Babylonia in the 14th century B.C. A hundred years later, they had occupied most of Syria and Phoenicia. But in the 10th century the Aramaeans drove them back.

A Hittite statue from Tal Halaf in Aleppo dates from the ninth century B.C.

EMPIRES

In the eighth century B.C., the Assyrians returned and conquered all of Syria, ending the separate historical development. However, this empire did not last long. In the seventh century B.C., King Nebuchadnezzar led the Babylonians to conquer the land. A hundred years later, Syria became part of the Persian Empire. Then, in 333 B.C., Alexander the Great conquered it, and it remained a Greek outpost until the Romans under Pompey added Syria to the Roman Empire in 64 B.C.

The period of Roman rule was prosperous and much building was accomplished. The Romans left the largest number of remains in Syria: cities, amphitheaters, temples, and forts from Turkey to Jordan and from the Mediterranean coast to the Euphrates River. Damascus became famous for its architecture and its schools of law and medicine. Palmyra, a trading center for caravans, reached its height in the mid-third century A.D.

In A.D. 395 the Roman Empire split in half. Syria became part of the eastern, or Byzantine, empire. The Byzantine rulers, who were Christian, tried to convert the Syrians but were successful only in the north.

There were three Roman emperors who came from Syria. One was Philip, who ruled the empire from A.D. 244 to 249. His birthplace of Shahba has ruins of a Roman theater, Roman baths, and a museum of well-preserved mosaic floors. The other two emperors, Alexander (Lucius) Severus (193–211), and Elagabalus (218–222), came from Homs (called Emesa at that time), 100 miles (161 km) north of Damascus.

Ruins of an aqueduct at Palmyra. The Romans destroyed Palmyra in A.D. 272.

Zenobia in Chains, an 1859 sculpture by Harriet Hosmer.

QUEEN ZENOBIA

Smack in the middle of Syria, about 150 miles (241.4 km) from the nearest city, stand the ruins of Palmyra, an extensive and beautiful Roman city that was built in the early third century A.D. In A.D. 260 a man named Odenathus was given the title "king of Palmyra" by the Roman emperor. His wife's name was Zenobia, and little is known about her before she married him, except that she was one of the best-educated women of her time and was an expert linguist. There are rumors that she was half Arab and half Greek—but this has not been confirmed.

Odenathus died in 267, and it is suspected that Zenobia had a hand in his death. Zenobia proclaimed herself queen, although she was officially acting as regent for her baby son. For a while, she appeared to defend Roman interests in the area, but starting in 268 she embarked on a conquest for herself. Her armies took over all of Syria, ventured into Egypt in 269, and by 270 had conquered all of Asia Minor, building fortifications at strategic points to defend her realm. In 270, Aurelian was elected the new Roman emperor, and at about the same time, Zenobia proclaimed her still-infant son, Septimius Vaballathus Athenodorus, emperor.

Aurelian became alarmed at the ambitions of Zenobia and sent a trusted general to recapture Egypt. He himself went after the queen of the desert, defeating her army in Antioch (now Antakya,

Turkey) and at Emesa (now Homs, Syria) in 271. He then reached Palmyra, which Zenobia defended for some time; but the city eventually surrendered and was razed by his troops in 273.

Legend claims that Zenobia and her son were captured by Roman soldiers as they fled Palmyra, and when the soldiers wanted to kill her, she saved her life by blaming her ministers and allowing them to be executed in her place, including one who had been her linguistic tutor. Whatever it was, Aurelian marched triumphantly back to Rome in the year 274 with the rebel queen in tow on a golden chain, bound with golden shackles, and covered with expensive jewelry. Some say she married a Roman senator and lived out the remainder of her life in a villa at Tibur (now Tivoli). Aurelian also pardoned her son and married her daughters into influential Roman families.

Zenobia is an important figure for many Syrian women. When Syrian men say a woman should only do certain kinds of work, that she cannot lead a country or an army, many women counter with, "What about our Queen Zenobia?" Even though her reign was short, she challenged the world's largest empire and held off its armies for several years. Perhaps equally important, she was successful in defeat, earning the respect of the very people she had tried to outdo.

A sculpture from Palmyra made during the reign of Zenobia.

The Omayyad Mosque is one of the oldest in the world and is still functioning today.

THE OMAYYADS

Although all of the civilizations and empires left their mark on Syria in some way, it was the zeal of Islam that changed it permanently and formed the basis of modern Syrian society.

After the Prophet Mohammed's death, his followers were divided over who should lead them. The Shia Muslims argued that it must be a member of the Prophet's family and chose Ali, the Prophet's son-in-law. The majority of followers, the Sunnis, wanted to elect caliphs to rule in his place. Immediate animosity developed between the two groups and continues today.

In addition to this split, there were conflicts between clans struggling for political and religious power. The Omayyads were initially the strongest of these clans. Led by Khalid ibn al-Walid, they conquered Damascus in 636, and most of the population adopted Islam.

The Omayyads ruled most of the Arab empire from Damascus, from the mid-seventh to the mid-eighth centuries. They continued in their drive to spread Islamic rule and eventually extended the Arab empire to include the entire Arabian Peninsula, northern Africa as far as the Atlantic Ocean, and southern Europe—an area about the same size as the former Roman Empire.

After the Omayyads took over in the seventh century A.D., Arabic spread as the common language

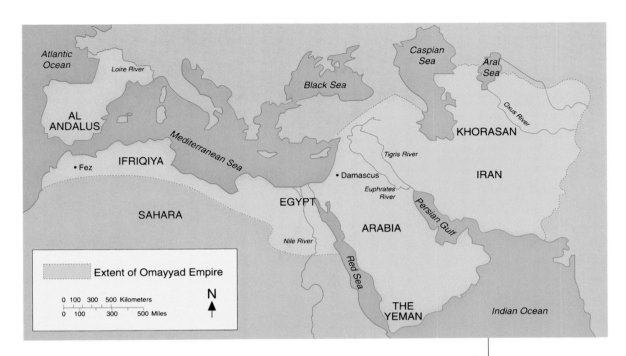

Extent of Omayyad Empire

0 100 300 500 Kilometers
0 100 300 500 Miles

N

of the land. Although Christianity had strongholds in the mountains of western Syria, the only religion that was able to take hold uniformly was Islam, and it has had an overriding influence on the country's development and direction. Adherents of other religions were, however, allowed to continue to practice their religion.

The Omayyads built roads, founded hospitals, and encouraged education. Scholars from other lands studied in Damascus, developing new medical practices and philosophical ideas. The Omayyad Empire is considered to be a high point of early Islamic civilization.

Under the Omayyads, however, political administration, education, intellectual pursuits, and other aspects of city life were more highly valued than rural life. This caused conflict between the predominantly rural inhabitants of the Middle East and the urban dwellers. That conflict, combined with the strife between Sunni and Shia groups and among clans, finally overwhelmed the Omayyads around the middle of the eighth century. Muslims based in Baghdad, with the support of Shia Muslims, conquered the area but neglected the coastal areas, which fell under the control of Egypt.

The first Arabs left a landmark, the lovely Omayyad Mosque in Damascus. This was built in the seventh century over the ruins of the Cathedral of Saint John, which in turn had been built over a Roman temple. It contains a sepulcher that Muslims believe holds the head of John the Baptist.

25

The siege of Damascus during the Second Crusade is illustrated in the late 15th-century French manuscript *Conqueror of Jerusalem.*

THE CRUSADERS

During the 10th and 11th centuries, Greater Syria devolved into many local principalities and emirates, and this political fragmentation allowed invading French Crusaders to take over much of northern and western Syria. The Crusaders came in waves, building mighty hilltop fortresses that still stand. A primary focus of the battle between the Crusaders and the Muslims and Jews was for control of Jerusalem, which was a holy city to all of them.

Despite their success on the coastal plains and in the coastal mountains, however, the Crusaders never had much impact in central and eastern Syria, and the cities of Damascus, Homs, and Hama were never taken.

In 1169 the Syrian sultan Nureddin sent his general Salah al-Din (commonly called Saladin) to the Egyptian royal court. Saladin took control of Egypt in 1171 and after Nureddin's death became sultan of both Egypt and Syria. He attacked the Crusaders and forced the European armies out of Jerusalem in 1188.

THE OTTOMANS

Approximately 300 years after the Crusaders were driven out, the Turkish Ottomans took over the land and probably had the strongest influence on modern Syria. They brought a certain amount of material success to the land and were Sunni Muslims like most Syrians. They allowed local administration by Arabs who were at least nominally loyal to them. These Arabs were wealthy landowners with deep roots in cities such as Damascus and Aleppo. The Ottomans ruled for about 400 years, until the end of World War I.

The Azem Palace in Damascus was the 18th-century residence of a Turkish governor.

INDEPENDENCE

After the Turks were driven out of Syria, France and England competed for the spoils. They both had political, religious, and economic reasons for wanting a presence in the area. France finally won control of Syria.

Syria rebelled against French rule from 1925 to 1927, but was crushed by superior military power, including a French bombardment of Damascus. The Syrians continued unsuccessfully to fight for their independence until Article 78 was adopted by the new United Nations in June 1945. It stated that members of the United Nations could not be placed under occupation by another country. The Arab League declared that the presence of French and British forces in the Levant violated the countries' sovereignty. Finally, after a lot of wrangling and hostilities, French troops left Syria on April 17, 1946. This is called Evacuation Day, which is a national holiday today.

A DIFFICULT START

Syria started its new life as an independent country with enormous problems. In 1947 the United Nations awarded a part of Palestine, which in Ottoman times was part of Greater Syria, to the Zionist Jews of Europe, in opposition to the wishes of the Arab majority in the area and of the neighboring Arab countries. There was almost immediate fighting between Israel and the Arab states, including Syria.

In addition, Syria's economy was weak. Few roads or railroads were built under the French occupation, and the poor land and harsh climate of the new country made self-sufficiency difficult. The lushest, most fertile parts of the Levant now formed the new countries of Lebanon and Israel or had been given to Turkey before World War II. Syria was left with arid lands more suitable for grazing than farming.

A Syrian woman holding the Syrian flag in Kuneitra, near the Golan Heights.

The difficulties Syria inherited resulted in a series of military coups from the very beginning of independence. The threat of military takeover has continued to plague Syria to the present day.

In 1958 Syria and Egypt tried to put Pan-Arabism—the belief that all Arab people should be part of one nation—into action. Pan-Arabism has been an Arab ideal since the early 20th century. Their effort at confederation, the United Arab Republic, was, however, short-lived. Egypt completely dominated Syria, and the union disintegrated in 1961.

In the mid-1960s, a group of dissident military officers came to power through the growing and powerful Baath Party, a Pan-Arab party in Syria and Iraq. The Baath Party was founded by two schoolteachers from Damascus, one Christian and one Muslim. Inspired by the new spirit of nationalism, the unifying factor was not religious belief but the oppression of Arabs. The Baath Party itself was strongly socialistic, which appealed to the Syrian masses; they were tired of the Sunni aristocrats, who had cooperated with the Ottomans for centuries, enhancing their own wealth and power.

In 1970 Hafez Al Asad, then Minister of Defense, organized a bloodless military coup. He ruled from 1971 until his death in 2000, when his son, Bashar, succeeded him. President Bashar Al Asad has begun to open dialogue with government opponents and mend bad relations with other countries in the region, such as Lebanon and Turkey.

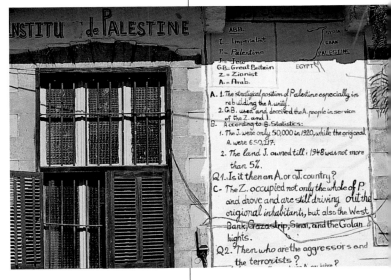

Arguments for Palestinian independence on the front wall of the Institute of Palestine in Damascus. Syria takes a great interest in the fate of Palestine.

Syria's recent history has been plagued by repeated wars with Israel that have drained the country's resources.

GOVERNMENT

SYRIA'S OFFICIAL NAME is the Syrian Arab Republic, and its capital is Damascus. All citizens can vote for both the president and the members of the legislative assembly.

GOVERNMENT STRUCTURE

In 1971 Hafez Al Asad (*al asad* means "the lion" in Arabic) was elected president by an assembly of his own choosing. The constitution, established in 1973, gave the president almost total control of the country. When President Hafez died in 2000, the Baath Party nominated his son, Bashar, for president. In the 2000 elections, Bashar ran uncontested and was duly elected with 97.29 percent of the vote. Presidential elections are held every seven years with the next vote scheduled for 2007. The president is head of state.

The prime minister is head of the government and is appointed by the president. The president also appoints a Cabinet of Ministers of varying size. In addition, there is a People's Council of 250 seats. Elections are held every four years with the last in 2003 and the next in 2007. The Baath Party is guaranteed half of the seats by the 1973 constitution. All adults can elect councillors and independent (non-Baath) representatives currently control 83 seats (33 percent of the council). A number of seats are reserved for farmers and workers. Women are guaranteed equality in elections and about 10 percent of the council and 5 percent of ministers are women.

The People's Council proposes laws, debates cabinet programs, and approves the national budget. The council can override presidential vetoes by a two-thirds majority but has never done so. Although the constitution requires that the president be a Muslim, there are no religious qualifications for the assembly.

Opposite: **A statue of Hafez Al Asad at Asad Dam. According to official government statistics, President Asad received 99.9 percent of the vote in the 1991 election; no one has ever run against him.**

The ruling Baath Party proposes the candidate for president and he is then nominated by the legislative branch, the People's Council. After the nomination process, the candidate is confirmed by a popular referendum.

A political banner displays Hafez Al Asad's picture. Even though the government now allows citizens to grumble openly, it tolerates no organized opposition.

THE BAATH PARTY

In Arabic, *baath* means "resurrection" or "renaissance" and refers to the party's origin as a movement in support of Arab unity and nationalism. The party was founded after World War II and gained strength when Palestinian lands were given to European Jews to form Israel. Baathists felt that the lack of Arab unity had made this possible.

The 1973 constitution established the Baath Party as the "leading party of the state and society." It currently dominates the alliance of seven political parties known as the National Progressive Front (NPF) that controls Syrian politics with 67 percent of the seats in the People's Council and the right to name presidential candidates. While other parties exist, Baathists effectively control the government, most media, and the military.

THE LEGAL SYSTEM

Syria's system of justice is based on the French model. There are civil and criminal courts. Lawsuits and other civil cases often take years to settle.

The State Security Court is only for political opponents the government accuses of being "security risks." Trials in this system violate most international standards for fair trials.

Courts governing personal status, such as birth, marriage, and inheritance, are divided according to religion. For Muslims, there is a court that follows the Muslim code, called the *Sharia*. There are separate courts for Druze, Roman Catholics, Orthodox believers, Protestants, and Jews.

THE MILITARY

Syria is widely regarded as a country with serious human rights problems. Al Asad Senior was known to use arbitrary imprisonment and torture to suppress opposition to his rule. His son, Bashar, has begun to relinquish control and has periodically released political prisoners as a gesture of tolerance to those who oppose the government.

The armed forces are divided into the army, navy, and air force, with the police and security forces maintaining domestic control. The country maintains a large armed force in part because it has been at war on and off with Israel for decades and in part because it has had to use force to suppress dissident movements at home.

Military service lasting 24 months is compulsory for men between 18 and 40 years of age. Exceptions are made in cases where the man is the only son in the family and for those with serious medical condition. Students may postpone their military service while completing post-secondary education. Syrian men who have lived abroad and middle- to upper-class youths eligible for draft usually buy an exemption out of military service for about $5,000.

After years of occupying Lebanon amid international condemnation, Syria recalled its troops in 2005 and reduced compulsory military service from 30 to 24 months. President Al Asad's new openness to reform may lead to a less militarized society in the long run.

A soldier standing below a poster of President Bashar Al Asad in Damascus.

ATTITUDES TOWARD GOVERNMENT

Bakshesh *(buk-SHEESH), a bribe or tip, is common, from paying a traffic officer to avoid a ticket to buying a favor from a party or government official. Smuggling in consumer products is a major industry with* bakshesh *paid to customs and military officials for their assistance.*

At gatherings in Syria, politics is often the chief topic of conversation. Most Syrians have a strong libertarian streak and are wary of any government. Particularly in rural areas, people generally believe that the government does not understand their problems. In urban areas regional jealousies have created tensions with the government. Currently there is a feeling among other groups that the government favors Alawites.

Although the government is unpopular with some groups—mostly the fundamentalist Muslims and the old-time aristocrats—there is some support for it among common people and some religious minorities. The people who support the government are those who have benefited socially, politically, or financially or who feel that a secular government protects the diverse religious practices in Syria better than one that imposes religious beliefs as law. While Westerners are sometimes appalled at the lack of certain freedoms, the tradition of strong, autocratic leaders is deeply rooted in modern Arab political culture.

NATIONALISM AND GREATER SYRIA

Rivalry among the country's various religious and ethnic minorities has been an ongoing source of instability in Syria. National loyalty traditionally takes second place to religious and ethnic loyalties, so the government appears at times to Syrians to represent no more than another faction among factions.

In the years since independence, however, an intense patriotism has developed, along with a strong desire for the recovery of what Syrians feel are integral areas of Syria split off from the nation by French authorities. These areas include Hatay Province, which is now part of Turkey, the whole of Lebanon, and the Golan Heights. The return of the Golan Heights, which was taken by Israel in the 1967 war and annexed in 1981, has been a Syrian condition of peace with Israel.

Many Syrians advocate the wider goal of restoring Greater Syria. Greater Syria is considered to encompass present-day Syria, Lebanon, Jordan, and Israel or Palestine. For this reason, Syria has taken a direct interest in Lebanon and maintained troops there until 2005.

The Baath Party also reflects the viewpoint of many Syrians in championing Pan-Arab nationalism. It advocates the unification of all Arab countries into one nation that would include all of the Middle East and North Africa. Pan-Arab nationalism regards the borders established by Ottoman or European rulers as arbitrary and artificial, and bases its call for unity on the shared heritage of Arabic language and culture.

Above: **Pro-Khomeini graffiti on the wall of a mosque. Some Muslim fundamentalist groups oppose the government because it is secular.**

Opposite: **The Golan Heights were annexed by Israel in 1981. All Syrians except the Druze were expelled from the area and Israeli settlers were moved in.**

ECONOMY

SYRIA IS A MIDDLE-INCOME, developing country. Although there is poverty and only a few people are wealthy, the number of middle- and upper-class people has grown in recent years. Government price controls on basic items allow even the poorest people to survive. The country is not rich in oil like countries in the Persian Gulf, but it does produce some oil and is engaged in major exploration for more.

The Syrian economy has expanded slowly but steadily in the last few years despite slowing oil production and continued government subsidies on key products. The new president has relaxed some of the restrictions, allowing private banks to open for the first time, unifying exchange rates, and raising some prices on basic foods. Foreign companies have also been invited to explore for oil to increase the production of this vital resource.

Twenty years ago Syria was overwhelmingly an agricultural country. Today its economy is divided among industry, mining, and agriculture.

Opposite: **A view of the city of Damascus.**

Left: **A family works together on a farm.**

37

Threshing grain. Syria has had to import some grain in recent years.

AGRICULTURE

In the 1970s, 50 percent of the population was involved in farming; in the 1980s this figure had fallen to 30 percent where it remains today. Agriculture contributes about 25 percent of the gross domestic product (GDP). Wheat, barley, cotton, legumes like chickpeas and lentils, fruit, vegetables, and sheep are the mainstays of farming.

Syria is nearly self-sufficient in basic food products. It produces a large amount of chicken and lamb, and some beef. Its primary vegetables and fruits are chickpeas, lentils, tomatoes, potatoes, onions, cucumbers, cabbage, beans (both dried and green), squash, eggplant, artichokes, peas, corn, parsley, lettuce, melons, peaches, pears, pomegranates, prickly pears, apples, figs, dates, grapes, olives, and pistachios.

The southwestern corner of the country might be called the nation's breadbasket, because this is where most of the wheat is grown. Tobacco has recently been introduced into this area to augment the wheat, melons, corn, prickly pears, pomegranates, and grapes already produced there.

MINING AND MANUFACTURING

Mining contributes 14 percent of the GDP. Petroleum alone accounts for almost 60 percent of total export earnings. The main fields are at Qaratshuk, Suwaydiya, and Rumaylan in northeastern Syria and at Deir-ez-Zor in eastern Syria. Syria also has some phosphates, natural gas, and iron ore.

Industry accounts for 31 percent of the GDP and employs 27 percent of the workforce. Mining industries contribute 61 percent of the industrial total, while manufacturing accounts for 34 percent and power generation for 5 percent. The main industrial products are petroleum and its by-products (fertilizers and plastics, for example), textiles and clothing, processed foods and beverages, leather products like footwear, and tobacco products. The textile industry is varied and extensive. Locally grown cotton is spun into thread at factories in Aleppo, Hama, and Damascus. Cotton, wool, and handmade silk are also manufactured.

EXPORTS AND IMPORTS

Syria's primary exports are oil, cotton (grown mostly around the Euphrates River), vegetables, fruit, and textiles. There are also a growing number of import-export businesses that export such things as food and industrial products. Exports have doubled from about $3.5 billion in the early 1990s to over $6 billion today.

Over the same time period, imports have grown more slowly from $4.1 billion in 1993 to $5 billion. The main imports are machinery and transportation equipment, electrical generation equipment, food, livestock, metal products, chemicals, plastics, yarn, and paper.

An oil pipeline brings crude oil to refineries in the western part of the country.

EMIGRATION

Syria, like some other less-developed countries, suffers a "brain drain." Doctors, dentists, and pharmacists, who include many of the brightest students, often go abroad to study and never return. Engineers, after they have served their five years working for the government, also often leave to find better pay elsewhere. The most common destinations for these emigrants are the oil-rich Gulf countries, North America, and Europe—usually in that order.

On the other hand, remittances sent home from Syrians working abroad have contributed toward Syria's finances. Any drop in payments caused by workers having to return home adversely affects the balance of payments.

Selling fish in Latakia.

JOBS

With few exceptions, Syrians are able to pursue whatever livelihood they choose. One exception is that an engineering graduate must work five years after graduation for a government agency before going into private practice or obtaining a better job with private industry or outside the country. Family and social pressures and economic realities, however, often dictate what career a young person pursues, despite the official freedom of choice.

Unfortunately, freedom of choice does not guarantee a job and about 20 percent of Syrians are officially unemployed. Those who are lucky enough to find work in the largely state-controlled business world make about $100 per month, which is hardly generous. Even professional jobs like engineering or being a university professor do not pay very well, which means that inequality and the income divide is not as dramatic here as in countries like Mexico or Egypt. Nonetheless many Syrians are frustrated at the lack of growth in the private sector that President Bashar Al Asad promised when he came to power in 2000.

With a little family inheritance, maybe a small shop, and several salaries, families get by. Bus and taxi fares, medical fees, and the prices on locally produced food, clothing, and medicine are among the lowest in the world.

A DAY IN THE LIFE

With such low salaries, how do Syrians survive?

The government has strict rent control laws that help families afford their living quarters. Young people whose families have money assist them until their incomes are adequate. Nearly everyone holds two or three jobs. A man might work as an electrical engineer for the government in the morning, sell electrical equipment to hospitals for a European company in the early afternoon, and work in his video rental store until 9 or 9:30 P.M. Millions of Syrians follow a similar pattern. In addition many people participate in unofficial currency exchanges with foreigners or smuggling. Finally families pool their incomes, and young people rarely leave home before marriage (and often stay for several years after they marry).

OPENING UP THE ECONOMY

From the coup in the mid-1960s up to the mid-1980s, Syria's economy was highly centralized. All utilities, transportation, and heavy industry were owned and operated by the government. Small merchants and craft workers, professional people, farmers, and shepherds were free to operate their own means of livelihood, but with price controls.

About the time that the Soviet Union—a long-time patron of Syria—began to look for ways to decentralize economic control, so did Syria. Investment Law 10, a 1991 directive issued by the president, liberalized economic restrictions and encouraged private investment in certain commercial and industrial areas. The government, however, remains the country's utilities manager. It heavily subsidizes public transportation, sets prices on fuel and basic foods, and operates most heavy industries.

The traditional *norias* (NOH-ree-ahs), or water wheels, have long provided irrigation to Syria's farmland. Lack of water is a major reason for economic problems.

President Bashar Al Asad promised reforms and privatization in the economy and has been able to make a few small changes like allowing private banks to open and reducing some subsidies on food to help farmers earn their livings. But change has been slow. There are pros and cons to the wholesale privatization of the economy and Syrians know this. On the positive side, overly bureaucratic and inefficient government industries would be replaced with leaner private ones that could attract foreign investment. On the downside, Syrians would lose the many price controls that make subsistence possible for the majority.

ECONOMIC PROBLEMS

The death of Hafez Al Asad in 2000 opened a window of opportunity for economic and political reform. His son Bashar brought a new optimism to the country when he announced that he would give Syrians more freedom to do business and to speak their minds. His ideas ran counter to the traditional state elite who wanted to maintain the status quo, but he had popular support and so was able to implement a few changes.

Unfortunately, war in Iraq disrupted regular economic flows of oil and tourists, and left Syria isolated. This has allowed the conservative elite to argue that Syria needs to retain tight economic controls and has prevented further liberalization.

Syria also faces problems in its oil sector where output from old wells is declining and the government is having a hard time getting international companies interested in exploring for new supplies given the instability in the region. In that sense, Syria's future is very much tied to the future of the Middle East as a whole.

New construction and television advertising are booming, and signs of prosperity are everywhere. Unfortunately poverty, crime, and Western-style materialism are also on the rise.

ENVIRONMENT

SYRIA IS NOT THE FIRST PLACE that comes to mind when you think about nature's bounty or diversity. As an arid region that has been inhabited by humans for thousands of years, it is not surprising that there is not an abundance of wildlife.

The Syrian plains and mountains used to host a wide array of animals, such as cheetahs, leopards, and ostrich, but almost all large animals have been hunted or driven from their habitats to the point of extinction.

Syria's cities have been polluted by industrial activity and the use of low-grade fuels, and its plains are subject to soil degradation caused by poor irrigation practices and wind erosion. However, a new approach is taking hold. From the government to the youngest citizens, Syrians are reclaiming and rehabilitating their natural environment.

URBAN PROBLEMS

The main causes of air pollution in Syria's cities are diesel-powered vehicles, domestic heaters, and large factories. Cities such as Damascus rely on a large fleet of micro-buses to move people around. These buses run on a low grade of diesel fuel that Syria refines from its own oil supplies. This fuel is a major pollutant, but micro-bus owners cannot afford to upgrade their engines and vehicles. Also, there is little unleaded gasoline produced in Syria, so newer vehicles have trouble finding sources of fuel.

In the colder months of November through March, Syrians heat their homes using small diesel heaters that are cheap to buy and operate. Using the same dirty fuel as the buses, heaters are the second biggest contributor to air pollution in the country.

Opposite: **A shephard watching over his sheep by the cliffs in northern Syria.**

Below: **Smog over the city of Damascus.**

A stonemasonry factory discharging waste into a river in Damascus.

"I love the environment class. It teaches us how we can maintain the environment. If I see children throwing rubbish on the ground, I pick it up immediately and put it in a bin."
— *Rasha al-Zenji, 9-year-old participant in the SEA-Movimondo Project.*

Running a close third are oil refineries and processing plants in cities like Homs, Banias, and Damascus. As Syria industrialized, no restrictions were placed on the location of heavy industry, therefore much of it is found in residential and office areas. Heavy industry is not regulated, so oil refineries, petrochemical and cement producers, and other such plants pump their waste into the cities' water sources, causing water pollution. They also emit toxic fumes and bury solid waste in open spaces.

INTERNATIONAL PARTNERS FOR CHANGE

In the mid-1990s the Syrian government joined with the United Nations Development Program and the World Bank to devise a strategy for formulating environmental policies and enforcing them. Since then, other countries, such as Italy and Germany, have become involved in helping the government and people of Syria address their environmental problems.

The German national development agency (GTZ) is working with Syria's Ministry of State for Environmental Affairs (formed in 1979) to provide information on air pollution in Damascus. They are monitoring traffic junctions across the city to figure out when and where pollution is highest. This information will help the government design solutions such as more environmentally friendly public transportation and lower tariffs on green technology including solar panels for home heating and vehicles with catalytic converters. The GTZ is also providing information to small- and medium-size industries on how to operate more efficiently and recycle waste. One of the byproducts of information sharing is the development of a new industrial zone south of Damascus and away from residential areas.

Cooperation between nongovernmental organizations (NGOs) is also having an effect. The Syrian Environment Association (SEA) and Movimondo of Italy have teamed up to spread environmental awareness among schoolchildren in the old city of Damascus. Environmental education programs encourage children to take an active role in keeping their city and its parks clean, as well as to learn about recycling glass, paper, and plastic. The children are encouraged to put on plays that demonstrate environmental principles. The hope is that children will bring their newfound knowledge home and encourage their families to adopt more environmentally friendly behavior. The program has been so successful that there are plans to expand it to other parts of Damascus and to other cities.

Mounds of scrap metal and factory waste waiting to be recycled in the Ghouta Plain.

RURAL PROBLEMS: SALINIZATION IN THE EUPHRATES VALLEY

Syria has long depended on irrigation to grow crops. However, if water is not drained away from the surface efficiently, mineral salts in the soil dissolve in the water. When the water evaporates, the salts are left on the surface of the soil, and the soil becomes salinized. Very few plants will grow in salinized soil.

The area around Aleppo was converted to cotton production in the 1950s after large-scale diesel-fuelled irrigation systems were built there. By the 1960s a lot of land was too salt-laden to produce any crops and had to be abandoned. Using deeper drainage systems, some of this land is being brought back into cultivation. After washing the land, barley can be grown for a few years before other crops are introduced.

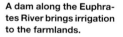

A dam along the Euphrates River brings irrigation to the farmlands.

SOIL EROSION ON THE STEPPE

The eastern part of the country, called the steppe, or Badia, is used mostly by nomadic and semi-nomadic sheep herders. The main environmental problem in this region is the loss of soil to wind erosion. Even light winds can carry sand and dirt away if the land is not protected by plant cover. The main causes of this problem are overgrazing and the use of heavy trucks for transportation of water, food, and animals.

Herders move their animals around according to seasonal rainfall and plant growth patterns. Traditionally, arid zones such as the Syrian steppe were not harmed by this, but changes in the last half century have taken their toll. In 1950 there were about 2.6 million sheep grazing in the steppe; today there are 10 to 12 million sheep—almost five times more. Shepherds have been able to increase their flocks because the government has provided subsidized feed for the animals and has not enforced restrictions on when and for how long different areas can be grazed.

The herders have used certain types of bushes and shrubs for fuel and medicine for millennia, but as their population increased, this practice

"Hopefully, they (Syrians) will become proud of this rare bird still surviving in their country and the northern bald ibis will become the symbol of a new conservation concern in Syria."
—Gianluca Serra, Palmyra Project, Talila Reserve.

has started to have a negative impact on the environment. The traditional practice of uprooting plants rather than harvesting branches meant that the soil was exposed to the force of wind erosion. In the same way, large vehicles chew up the crusty layer on top of the soil, exposing the earth beneath to erosion.

The Syrian government, together with the United Nations Food and Agriculture Organization (FAO) and the Italian government, initiated the Rangeland Rehabilitation and Establishment of a Wildlife Refuge Project in 1996. The project reseeded a few hundred acres of steppe with native plants and established an education center for visitors and locals to learn more about steppe conservation. The highlight of the project was the establishment of the Al Talila Reserve about 18.6 miles (30 km) east of Palmyra.

MIRACLES DO HAPPEN

The northern bald ibis was believed to be extinct in Syria and most of the Mediterranean region. The last sightings in Syria were in 1928 and the last wild breeding colony died out in Turkey in 1989. The only known populations of these birds were those raised in captivity in Turkey and a few hundred wild animals living in Morocco.

Then in 2002, Gianluca Serra, an Italian working with the Al Talila project, heard rumors from local hunters and herders that birds matching the ibis's description had been sighted nearby. Using a questionnaire and photos of ibises and related species, Serra and her Syrian colleagues began a systematic survey of the region. After two years they finally found the nesting site of three pairs and a seventh adult bird.

The northern bald ibis is a migratory bird that needs wild or semi-wild areas where it can find its favorite foods of insects, young frogs, and snakes while it nests and raises its young. Humans disrupt this habitat when they farm or draw too much water from rainy-season ponds, destroying the breeding grounds of the ibis's prey. Despite the grim statistics of extinction in this region, the ibis proves that miracles do happen.

AL TALILA RESERVE

Syria's first and only wildlife refuge, Al Talila, officially opened in 2003. It is small with 2,470 acres of land, but its significance is enormous. By fencing off the reserve from grazing domestic animals, this area shows how productive well-maintained land can be. Endangered Arabian oryx and gazelles were imported from Saudi Arabia to repopulate the land. In just a few years, their numbers increased from eight to 13 oryx and 30 to 53 gazelles.

Biologists have been able to study steppe ecology here and have trained local Bedouin as nature guides. Syrian children come here on school trips to learn about their country's natural heritage. Scientists working in the reserve discovered a new species of beetle (*Aphodaulacus talilensis*), which was named after the reserve. Al Talila stands as a symbol for Syrians of what their country once was and could be again with careful management of human and natural needs.

An endangered Arabian oryx at the Al Talila reserve.

SYRIANS

SYRIA IS A COUNTRY OF extremely crowded cities and sparsely populated desert and steppe. Around 80 percent of the population lives within 80 miles (128.8 km) of the Mediterranean coast.

Syria may have the most diverse ethnic mix of any Arab country. Most Syrians are a mixture of ancient Phoenician, Babylonian, and Assyrian and more modern French and Turkish. Most consider themselves to be Arabs, a cultural, not a racial, category.

Although the majority of the people have olive-toned skin, dark brown eyes, and black hair, there is surprising variety in physical attributes. They range from blonde hair and very pale skin to a dark brown skin color with jet black hair. Quite a few Syrians have blue or pale gray eyes, usually with dark hair. Red hair and medium-brown hair are also commonly seen—sometimes accompanied by pale, freckled skin and brown eyes.

Above: **The** *souk*, **or traditional market, in Damascus.**

Opposite: **A Bedouin boy. Perhaps the only "pure" Arabs are the Bedouins.**

POPULATION FACTS

About 37 percent of the population is 14 years of age or younger and the population has grown rapidly in the last century. At the end of World War I, there were 200,000 Syrians; in 1972 there were 4.5 million; in 1986, 12 million, and in 2005, 18.4 million. The growth rate is 2.34 percent, compared to 0.92 percent for the United States.

Programs to eliminate illiteracy and changes in policies regarding the education of women have resulted in a sharp decline in fertility rates. Families are encouraged to send their girls to high school. Thus the average birthrate has fallen from eight children per family in the 1960s to three per family in 2005.

VARIED INFLUENCES

Syrian society includes a variety of social groups of various sizes that lack any set of shared values and loyalties that might bind the population into one nation. Differences in language, region, religion, ethnicity, and way of life produce a large number of separate communities, each with a strong internal loyalty and solidarity. One observer has spoken of the "empty center" of Syrian society, the lack of an influential group embodying a national consensus.

One reason for this fragmentation is the historical isolation of different groups. Christian groups have always played a prominent role in Syria, especially in the west and north. When the Omayyads first arrived, the various Christian groups, perhaps fearing persecution, moved farther into the mountains, forming separate communities. In later years, minority sects of Islam did the same. Under Egyptian rule, non-Muslim groups were given some autonomy. Under the Ottomans, the practice spread, creating what was called the Millet system: a system that gave Jewish and Christian communities their own governments within the empire.

Religious distinctions are psychologically and politically the most significant ones. Loyalty to one's religious group, rather than to the Syrian nation, is an important value. The religious communities are largely self-contained social systems that regulate much of the daily life of their members (*above, a Christian Syrian baking bread at the Saint Joseph Monastery*) and receive their primary loyalty.

In addition, language differences and differences in social organization between villagers, Bedouins, and city dwellers further fragment the society. Each of these groups practices a distinct, usually hereditary, way of life. Syria's post-independence history is largely the story of conflict between minority groups and the central government.

RACIAL AND CLASS CONSCIOUSNESS

In Syria, the lighter-skinned people usually dominate the top socio-economic positions and the darker-skinned people the bottom ones. Top government officials, business owners, and models in television commercials are almost uniformly lighter-skinned and often European in appearance, whereas construction workers, janitors, garbage haulers, and street cleaners are predominantly darker-skinned.

Although there is no violent racism, there seems to be a general feeling of superiority among lighter-skinned Syrians. Darker-skinned people are not considered to be the equals of this elite group. Bedouin nomads are also sometimes looked down upon despite the contribution of their culture to Arab identity.

Class consciousness is also very apparent. As in most countries, the rich and poor live separate lives and rarely meet socially.

Poor rural children. Educated city dwellers feel superior to illiterate villagers and rural people, and those who live in the cities of the western part of the country feel superior to those who live in the eastern part.

ETHNIC DIVERSITY

Arabs live in all parts of the country; non-Arab groups generally live in partial isolation from one another, either in their own village or cluster of villages, or in specific quarters of towns and cities.

KURDS The Kurds are believed to constitute about 9 percent of the population. Most live in the foothills of the Taurus Mountains north of Aleppo, in Al-Jazirah, near Jarabulus northeast of Aleppo, or in the Quarter of the Kurds on the outskirts of Damascus. They are a fiercely independent people with a deep pride in their history and traditions. Many arrived from Turkey between 1924 and 1938, in reaction to the Turkish attempt to suppress Kurdish culture by banning their language.

Kurds now live in the mountain regions of Turkey, Iraq, Iran, and Syria. Since the early part of this century, Kurds have been fighting for the independence of this region, which they call Kurdistan.

Kurds are traditionally nomadic herders and speak Kurdish, an Indo-European language. They are mostly Sunni Muslims.

Kurdish women do not wear the veil and enjoy considerable freedom, working and interacting socially with men. However, they are not encouraged to participate in political activities. In the villages women prepare food and clothing and bring water to the house. Men build the houses and take care of the animals. All help with the planting.

Dress varies for Kurdish women. Traditional dress for men consists of baggy pants bound at the ankles and worn with a tunic, vest, and cummerbund. They wear a brightly colored turban or yellow fur cap, and traditionally carry a curved dagger and rifle. Most Kurds, however, now wear European-style clothing, although their traditional dress remains a symbol of Kurdish unity, as does their appearance of fierceness.

There are about 1 million Palestinians living in Syria. Some are second-generation, and others were born in Israel. Palestinians are official residents and hold Syrian passports, but cannot vote. Most have assimilated well into Syrian society.

56

ARMENIANS Most of the Armenians in Syria arrived as refugees from Turkey between 1925 and 1945. They are city or town dwellers, with three-quarters living in Aleppo and another large group in the Quarter of the Armenians in Damascus. Many villagers in northwestern Syria are of Armenian descent. Armenians belong to the Armenian Orthodox Church or the Armenian Catholic Church. Their language is Armenian, an Indo-European language. They work chiefly in trade, the professions, small industry, or crafts and have a strong economic position, especially in Aleppo. They are the largest unassimilated group and retain many of their own customs, maintain their own schools, and read Armenian newspapers.

TURKS AND OTHER GROUPS The Turks are semi-nomadic herders in Al-Jazirah and along the Euphrates River, and farmers in the Aleppo area. Most have assimilated into Arab culture, but some still speak Turkish and retain ethnic traditions.

There are also small numbers of Circassians (descendents of Muslim nomads from the Caucasus), Assyrians, and Jews.

Brightly-colored dresses are typical of Kurdish women's clothing.

Saladin, the Islamic Empire's most successful commander, was a Kurdish officer in the Syrian army. He eventually became sultan of Egypt and Syria, and forced the Crusaders out of Jerusalem.

Syrian men may wear a headcloth similar to that worn in other Arab countries, or a checkered *kafeeyeh*.

MODE OF DRESS

It would be hard to find more diversity in dress anywhere else than in Syria. With such a large blend of cultures, every sect of Islam, both Eastern and Western Christianity, and disparate tribes from one corner of the country to the other, the clothing is often a treat for the eyes. A young woman wearing a white scarf and a raincoat (even in the burning heat of summer) can be seen arm-in-arm with her best friend—another young woman in tight blue jeans, with teased hair, heavy makeup, and loads of jewelry. A father in *kaftan* (a man's gown) and *kafeeyeh* (ku-FEE-yea), a wrapped cotton headdress, might be walking along with his sons, who are in blue jeans and T-shirts with English words printed on the front. An older woman, draped in black from head to foot, might be with her granddaughter, who is wearing colorful Syrian dress and earrings that look like small chandeliers. Many wealthy and educated Syrians dress similarly to Europeans or Americans. To add to this mix, every village and tribe of Bedouins has its own particular patterns, hand-embroidered designs, styles, and colors of clothing.

One item that symbolizes not only Middle Eastern dress, but Muslim dress in general, is the head wrap. In Syria there is an endless variety of materials, colors, textures, patterns, and styles of wrapping for both men and women. They range from elegant and gorgeous to torn, dirty, or sun-bleached.

Middle- and upper-class Syrian women, especially the younger ones, tend to wear bright colors, lots of jewelry and make-up, high-heeled shoes, and long hair teased and heavily sprayed, with "fountains" of hair cascading from the top. Young men of the middle and upper classes almost always have closely-cropped hair, and are also very dressy. Few middle- or upper-class Syrians wear jeans, T-shirts, running shoes, or other such casual attire.

Some things rarely seen in Syria are bare legs above the calves, bare shoulders or upper arms, shorts on adults (men or women), mini-skirts, short hair on women and girls, and long hair or earrings on men.

Average life expectancy is lower in Syria than in North America: 69 years for men and 71 for women. Nonetheless it has been improving steadily with increased access to medical care. The tendency for men to smoke heavily and the demands of childbirth for women are historically the causes of the lower life expectancy.

Typical women's attire would be a long dress and a head covering.

LIFESTYLE

SYRIANS HAVE their share of contradictions, making them simultaneously fascinating and frustrating. Although they are tremendously polite in their greetings and goodbyes, the less considerate ones may cut in line, jostle people so that they drop whatever they might be carrying, or frighten pedestrians by driving carelessly. Some taxi drivers and shopkeepers offer goods and services gratis as a welcome, but others may sometimes overcharge. Most people go out of their way to be hospitable, but they may also honk their horns incessantly, blast music, and talk loudly outside bedroom windows at midnight or 6 A.M.

Above: **It is common for men to put their arms around each other.**

Opposite: **A Syrian woman washing fleece by a stream.**

THE SYRIAN CHARACTER

Syrians love to laugh and joke, eat and talk, and dance. They love noise—loud music, hand clapping, car horns, loud voices—and few of them like peace and quiet at all. The younger ones have a tremendous amount of energy, even when in their mid-20s.

Theirs is a culture that strongly believes in fate, and that belief is reflected in the constant use of the expression *insha'Allah* (in-SHAH-al-LAH), meaning "God willing," whenever they talk about the future. It shows up in various other ways as well. They have a fatalistic sense of humor that is apparent in their political jokes. They do not monitor time and schedules. Being on time does not matter to them because whatever is going to happen is going to happen anyway!

61

Syrians are a sociable people, and their preference for a lot of company starts early.

SOCIAL INTENSITY

One thing a visitor to Syria quickly notices is the energy put into personal relationships. It is obvious on the streets and in homes, schools, and offices. When Syrian friends greet each other, their hellos and goodbyes seem endless. They ask about each other's families, work, school, and health, and "Where are you going?" or "Can you come have tea or ice cream with us?" Then they say goodbye in several ways and bestow blessings on each other. When they learn English, these habits come through in the new language, and they ask strangers how they are two or three consecutive times.

Along with social intensity comes physical closeness: male friends walk down the street arm-in-arm or holding hands; men hug and kiss other men, sometimes even on the lips; and women do the same with one another. Syrian friends touch each other constantly. Even engaged lovers and older married people often walk arm-in-arm or hand-in-hand, although this is not as common as physical contact between the same gender.

BEING PART OF THE GROUP

Syrians do not like to stand out from the crowd. Clannishness is part of their tradition: immediate family first, then clan or village (sometimes these are about the same), religion next, then nationality. The variety in dress is part of this group thinking—they dress as their group dresses.

Most Syrians do not like anything but their own cuisine. There is little variety in the naming of children. The most common first name for men is Muhammed. Many Muhammeds use their middle names for at least a little distinction. Other common men's names are Ahmad, Khalil, Khaled, Yassar, Imad, Samer, or one of a half dozen other widely used names. There is a slightly larger variety of women's names.

Syrians typically like to feel part of a group.

FAMILY ORIENTATION

Families are the absolute center of life in Syria, and this shows in many ways.

One of the first questions a foreigner in Syria gets asked is "Are you married?" If the answer is yes, the next question will be: "Do you have children?" If so, the Syrian will want to know all about the family. People here cannot understand children leaving home at the ages of 18, 19, or 20 (unless, of course, they get married), and they often make clear their belief that they are better parents than most Westerners—particularly North Americans. They point to things such as drug use, teenage pregnancy and suicide, and street kids as evidence that this is so. Most young people cannot imagine leaving their parents' homes when they are teenagers. Although some of them complain about the lack of privacy and family pressures, they generally think it is for the well-being of everyone. The idea of putting their aging parents in a nursing home is unacceptable to them (there are no nursing homes in Syria). Although some children are punished harshly at times, children and parents display a lot of affection toward each other.

Getting married and having children is the top priority for most Syrians. Children are so important (especially sons) that fathers and mothers traditionally use a different name after the first son is born. If they name the son Yassar, the father becomes Abu Yassar—literally "father of Yassar"—and the mother often becomes Umm Yassar—"mother of Yassar." If no sons are born, the mother usually identifies herself as the mother of the first-born daughter; fathers, however, rarely do this.

A Bedouin family in front of their tent. Family ties are guarded as a means of preventing loneliness as well as a source of support against the outside world in times of stress or danger. For most women, the home is the center of their lives.

*Despite the gradual
elimination of the
Bedouins' lifestyle,
some elements of
their culture live on,
in modified form,
in the daily lives of
some Arabs,
for example, the
segregation of men
and women,
arranged marriages,
clannishness, warm
hospitality, having a
strong and
autocratic leader,
and a strict code
of honor.*

THE PROTECTION OF THE CLAN

Clannish behavior in the Arab world developed from the harsh life of
the Bedouins. A hostile environment that required vast areas to support
a small amount of life led to the need for a strong sense of survival. An
individual alone was vulnerable to both the environment and other in-
dividuals or groups.

Therefore the tightest-knit kinship groups thrived the best. A man might
feud with his cousin or other relative, but when family members were
faced with any threat from outside (even if only perceived), absolute
unity was necessary.

Although most Arabs settled down as peasants and cultivators many
centuries ago, massive urbanization only took place within the past century. For thousands of years, the "law of the desert" and clan systems
ruled, thus the concept of allegiance to an extended family group became
second nature.

This clan loyalty heavily influences modern Arab politics, and who you
are related to can be as important as wealth, intelligence, and ability.

A traditional wedding party.

MARRIAGE

Arranged marriages are still very common in Syria, particularly among villagers and Bedouins. Even more modern city people often cannot choose who they want to marry; if they want a particular mate, both families usually have to agree on the arrangement. First cousins are still a preferred match. Among more modern Syrians, the father of a young woman may approach a young man he would like to see his daughter marry and ask if the young man is interested. Polygamy is legal for Muslims, although few urban Syrians practice it. Divorce is rare.

THE STORY OF A WEDDING DRESS

Bedouins and villagers are very traditional people. In many Syrian villages, a young woman's marital hopes are often expressed through the wedding dress she sews. The patterns of the dresses are set by village or clan tradition, although within those patterns each gown is slightly different. The traditional dress in most northern Syrian villages is heavy black material finely embroidered with scarlet patterns. The dress takes a year or longer to sew by hand and is often signed by the maker: her name is sewn into some part of the garment. The left side of the dress is often highly decorated, while the right side has only coarse, simple designs; this is because the baby is traditionally carried on the right arm. The woman usually wears the dress for several years.

A Western-style white wedding. Weddings are a particularly important occasion for Syrians.

Since marriage is the main goal in life, wedding parties are major social events. Among traditional people, the bride parties with her mother, sisters, female cousins, and friends in a house. They sing, dance, talk, laugh, and eat for hours. The bridegroom does the same with his male friends and relatives. The festivities may go on all night long in the city, all afternoon and evening in a village.

Wealthy people often rent a hotel ballroom or entire restaurant, and after some separate-gender celebration, the whole group may come together to eat, talk, and dance all night.

Depending on the custom of the area, the wedding party might take place either before the actual wedding or after it. Among the most traditional people, the families await confirmation from the groom, after the wedding night, that the new wife was a virgin. If she was not, or seems not to be, the marriage could be ended immediately and the woman severely punished by her family.

Two Syrian women enjoying a night of shopping in the city of Damascus.

WOMEN'S AND MEN'S ROLES

The constitution adopted at the founding of the Baath Party in 1947 stated: "The Arab woman enjoys all the rights of citizenship." This position sets Syria apart from most other Arab countries. Syrian women today enjoy full legal rights, and the government has promoted equal opportunities for women. Nonetheless, traditional restraints have prevented most women from taking advantage of these opportunities.

For more than 2,000 years, Arab culture considered women to be inferior and girls to be of less value than boys. Women are still viewed as weaker than men in mind, body, and spirit and therefore in need of male protection. The highly valuable and easily damaged honor of men depends largely on that of their women, especially on that of their sisters, so they are carefully protected. The slightest implication of unavenged impropriety on the part of the women in a family or of male infractions of the code of honesty and hospitality could irreparably destroy the honor of a family.

Despite traditionally being considered inferior to men, Syrian women today enjoy higher legal status than women in most other countries of the Middle East. They also have more freedom and are more respected compared to a few generations ago. There are women cabinet members and quite a few women in the Peoples' Legislative Assembly. However fewer than 10 percent of women work and only a handful have powerful positions.

DEATHS IN THE FAMILY

When someone dies, there are three days of mourning, during which friends, relatives, and neighbors visit the family. Close female relatives are expected to wear black for many months after the death. After a period of time, they can start wearing half black and half white. For very traditional families, it may be a year or longer before the women can wear colors again. For more modern families, the time is usually at least six months. If an older woman's husband dies and she is not likely to remarry, she may wear black for the rest of her life. These mourning traditions are similar in both Christian and Muslim families.

A person (especially a woman) who does not follow the mourning traditions is criticized for not having loved the deceased.

A Muslim must be buried within hours, clothed only in a shroud.

Above and opposite: **Schoolchidren going to school. Primary education is compulsory for six years. In 1991, 99 percent of primary school-aged children were enrolled, whereas only 45 percent of secondary school-aged children were in school.**

EDUCATION

Syria is striving to educate all its citizens, and literacy has increased dramatically in the last 20 years. Adult illiteracy has declined from 46.7 percent in 1980 to 23.1 percent in 2003. Syria has also made real progress combating female illiteracy, which has dropped from 66.2 percent in 1980 to 36.1 percent in 2003. School children attend school from 6 or 8 A.M. to 1 or 3 P.M. (depending on the season) six days a week. In high school, students are required to study a foreign language, either English or French, for two years.

Syria has four universities, and students pay only a token annual fee to attend. The largest is the University of Damascus, followed by the University of Aleppo. There are also universities in Latakia and Homs. The universities have huge classes and use outdated teaching and examination methods, so those who can afford to study abroad and get visas usually do so. There are also agricultural and technical schools for vocational training.

University students can study whatever they want with this exception: only the top percentage of high school students (based on special exams) are allowed to study medicine, and only the next best tier is allowed to study engineering. Neither group of students is required to study in those fields, but they usually do. This creates a situation where the brightest students are most often doctors, dentists, or engineers.

MOSQUE AND SCHOOL

Before there were schools in the Islamic world, there were mosques. Because Islam does not separate one part of life from any other, most Arab countries had no secular (that is, nonreligious) schools until the 20th century. Children were taught by the religious leader, or sheikh, who assured that their education was based on the teachings of the Koran and the life and teachings of the Prophet Mohammed. The Arabic name for mosque and university is from the same root: *jaamea*.

Today in Syria, most villages have secular schools. A few still use a mosque or church school, but the education is usually more focused on modern learning than it was in mosques of the past.

Many traditional Muslim leaders think mosque schools are the best way to assure that young people are taught proper behavior and beliefs. Muslims, however, are not the only religious group that believes in this. Where there are large populations of Armenians, there are Armenian Orthodox (Christian) schools that teach children their ancestral history, religion, and the Armenian language; and where there are concentrations of Jews, there are synagogue schools that teach children Jewish heritage and Hebrew.

A traditional beehive house in Ebla in northern Syria.

LIVING QUARTERS

All city dwellers live in apartments; many of them live in condominiums that are owned by the occupants. Syrian cities have no such thing as single-family homes, except for the mansions of ambassadors and top government officials. Many wealthy and upper-middle-class people build large vacation homes (called villas) in the mountains or near the sea. Some of these are relatively modest, but most are quite extravagant.

The focal point of rural houses is most often the front door. It may be huge compared to the house and is frequently decorated with geometric patterns and painted in multiple colors. In the western part of the country, nearly all rural houses are surrounded by olive trees and grapevines. Many houses have grape arbors over the roof to keep the hot summer sun off the house while at the same time creating favorable conditions to help ripen the grapes.

In the more traditional homes, the women and girls sit at one end of the room, while the men and boys sit at the other. If there is more than one main room, the genders may separate completely.

IN A SYRIAN HOME

The styles of decoration and furniture and the sizes of homes vary widely according to their owner's social class, religious background, and social attitudes. If there is a preferred decor in the homes of the middle- and upper-classes, it is an ornate Louis XIV style.

The chandeliers and other light fixtures truly stamp a place as Syrian. Many chandeliers are oversized for the rooms they light, sometimes hanging down below head-level. The brass frames are smothered with pieces of multi-faceted glass and when seen from the streets at night, often fill an entire window. Other lamps and light fixtures tend toward the ornate as well: brass floor lamps shaped as palm trees; table lamps glazed in pearlescent black or white with flowers, dolphins, or other decorations in brass-covered relief. All of this ornateness is enhanced by colorful French, Turkish, or Persian carpets and multicolored stone floors.

Many of the newer houses and those recently renovated feature modern European styles, accented with some Syrian embellishments. At the other end of the age spectrum lie the once grand houses of the ancient walled city of Damascus. These are hundreds of years old, each built around a courtyard with a fountain, citrus and eucalyptus trees, grapevines, and flowers. The ceilings are high to keep rooms cool during summer days.

The interior of a Muslim house in a rural area. It is common to sit on pillows on the floor, although there will also be other furniture.

73

*The old section
of a city houses
the groups that
have been there
the longest as well
as other groups
oriented toward
traditional life.
The souk is an
important feature
of the old city.*

A busy street in Damascus.

CITY LIFE

Half of the population of Syria lives in cities. The cities have several distinct sections. The ancient core of a city usually represents the pre-Greek or pre-Roman period, with sections added in Greek, Roman, and medieval times. The newer sections, often built by the French, house families who are more closely identified with modern technology and values.

Cities were traditionally organized into ethnic and religious residential quarters. Members of the different faiths still tend to live together, and the quarter functions as a small community within the larger urban setting. A residential quarter traditionally had its own mosque or other religious structure, shops, and coffeehouses where the men met, as well as a *mukhtar*, or mayor, who represented the group to the outside society. Within the quarter, family connections, personal reputation, and honor carried more weight than wealth.

Today many of the wealthier families live in the modern parts of the cities, where neighborhoods are divided along economic lines rather than by religious or ethnic affiliation. As a result, the old quarters have lost some of their leadership role, and the division between more traditional-minded people and the modernized middle classes has been accentuated.

VILLAGERS

Although more and more people from villages are finishing high school and even attending college, basic village life in Syria has not changed a lot over the centuries. Villages have less wealth than the cities; there are relatively few cars, and the ancient Arab cultural attributes are more noticeable here than in the cities. Villagers' lifestyles are closer to those of the Bedouins than to those of city dwellers. The villagers are less accustomed to foreigners and are more conservative. These traits are especially noticeable in villages in the desert and along the Euphrates River.

Most Syrian villages have electricity, some indoor plumbing, schools, and clinics, but these amenities are not universal. Where there is no official school, the local mosque or church serves as one.

In villages and rural areas, most people live in small, one- to three-room homes with a small courtyard, the older ones generally made from adobe bricks and plaster. Each village has a few villas built by villagers who have made money in the city or by local farmers who have been successful.

Village life is traditionally based on family and clan, summed up by the folk saying, "My brother and I against my cousin; my cousin and I against the outsider."

Bedouin women produce beautiful and often elaborate carpets, clothing, and jewelry. Even the full-time nomads usually have to augment their income from sheep with the sale of these craft items.

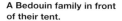

A Bedouin family in front of their tent.

BEDOUINS

Like indigenous peoples throughout the world, the traditional lifestyle of the Bedouins has changed a great deal and will probably disappear soon. This is not the result of colonialism, as it has been with most other indigenous peoples, but rather the result of the encroachment of modern living.

The traditional Bedouins' entire existence revolves around raising sheep and herding them from one sparse feeding ground to another in millennia-old seasonal cycles.

There are now three types of Bedouins: settled, semi-nomadic, and fully nomadic. The settled Bedouins live at the edge of the steppe or desert where there is enough water for them to grow crops. Semi-nomads spend winter in villages, and the rest of the year grazing their sheep. The fully nomadic groups live in their black goatskin tents all year, moving whenever they must to provide grazing for their sheep.

Two factors are destroying the traditional nomadic lifestyle. The first is modern technology in the form of trucks and tankers that haul sheep to market and water to sheep, circumventing natural watering holes and "sheep drives" to market. The second factor is the control that the government of Syria has gained during the last half a century over the tribal feuding and warfare that were common among clans for thousands of years. Now, instead of fighting with one another and keeping sheep to a level that allowed quick mobility, the Bedouins try to raise much larger flocks of sheep. In a fragile environment, these practices have caused severe overgrazing and have diminished the ability of the land to support sheep.

In the spring, when grazing is good in the desert and steppe, Bedouin tents are everywhere; and parked beside most of them is not a camel, but a large sheep-hauling truck and maybe even a generator. Many tents have televisions that run off the generator or truck. Children are often bussed to the village school.

Population growth and climate change have also contributed to the demise of traditional Bedouin life. Better healthcare has increased their lifespan at the same time that the land supports less life. Young Bedouins often end up in villages or cities where they farm, do construction work, clean streets, or do any other work they can find.

A Bedouin family. Women play a full part in Bedouin life, caring for the animals and setting up and dismantling the camps.

RELIGION

ALTHOUGH SYRIA HAS A LARGE assortment of religious groups, including Muslim, Christian, and Jewish, these groups all share a strong belief in God. Syrians' greetings, goodbyes, and many other common expressions give credit to God for everything, thank God for everything, and leave the future up to God. The most common response when you ask someone how he or she is, is *al Hamdulla* (al-HAM-dool-la), which means "Thank Allah!" When Syrians learn English, they translate these expressions into "God bless you," "God willing," and "Thank God." Although some of this may be only tradition without real feeling, it is hard to imagine most Westerners using similar expressions with such regularity. Religion is part of everyday life in Syria, and most people wear their beliefs proudly.

There are hundreds of churches in Syria, and all religions are guaranteed freedom of worship by the country's constitution. Syrian laws do not allow proselytizing—trying to convert others to your own religious beliefs. Perhaps for this reason, there has been less religious strife in Syria than in other countries with similarly diverse populations.

Muslims constitute about 90 percent of the population. Of this, 80 to 85 percent are members of the Sunni sect, 11 percent are Alawis, and approximately 1 percent are Ismailis. Other Shia groups constitute less than 1 percent of the population. Druzes, an offshoot of Islam, account for 3 percent of the population, and Christians for 10 percent. There are also small groups of Jews and Yazidis, a sect that combines elements of Judaism, Christianity, and Islam, as well as older religious beliefs.

Above: **A traditional religious man in the old quarter of Damascus.**

Opposite: **A girl reading the Koran in a religious class.**

ANCIENT RELIGIONS

Before the Muslim Omayyads conquered Syria in the eighth century, there had been many religions in the land. The Phoenicians, Assyrians, Babylonians, Greeks, and Romans all spread their own particular beliefs in different parts of Syria. The ancient beliefs were eventually replaced by the monotheism (belief in one God) of Judaism, Christianity, and Islam.

BAAL: WHOSE GOD WAS HE?

The name Baal (BAY-el) was first used in approximately the same sense Christians now use the word "Lord." Many gods were referred to as Baal among the Semitic people of the Middle East: the Sumerian god of the air, Enlil; Marduk, God of Babylon; Asshur, god of Assyria; and others. An Arabic expression for a polytheist—one who believes in more than one god—is *ashra baalla* (AHSH-ra BAAL-la), literally 10 gods. The Phoenicians initially used Baal as a title for their god of storms, Hadad, but it later became his name. Baal is an old word in both Hebrew and Arabic that means "husband," "master," and "owner." Baal Zebub, the healing god of Ekron, later became one word—Beelzebub—which came to represent evil and idolatry in the New Testament of the Bible.

One Canaanite myth claimed that Baal reigned during the growing season of the year, then died thereafter. His place was taken by Mot, meaning death, the god of death and sterility, who represented the hot, dry summers. Anat, who was Baal's wife and sister, searched for him during the reign of Mot, found him, and brought him back from death. That is how the autumn rains began.

Although the Hebrews purportedly believed only in Yahweh, they often adopted other "Baals" from the Canaanites. Jezebel, the Phoenician wife of King Ahab of the Hebrews, is an example of a Baal worshiper.

THE BEGINNING OF ISLAM

Although Judaism and Christianity are native to Greater Syria and have been there for thousands of years, Islam filled the land not only with its beliefs but also with the language of its holy book—the Koran—within a hundred years of its inception.

In 570 the Prophet Mohammed was born to a noble Arab family in Mecca, an area that was then called the Hejaz. He spent most of his life as a merchant, but it is said that when he was 40 years old and in solitary meditation, he was visited by the angel Gabriel. The angel began giving him God's words—in Arabic—which eventually became the Koran. Mohammed began spreading this new "revelation," attracting both followers and enemies among the people of Mecca. Hostility and persecution from the Meccans eventually forced him and his followers to flee to Medina in 622. This migration marks the beginning of the Muslim year. For eight years, Mohammed headed Islam from Medina, returning to Mecca in 630. Although he died two years later and was buried in Medina, Mecca became the most holy city for Muslims and the Kaaba Mosque its most holy place.

Early Islam was intensely expansionist. Conquering armies and migrating tribes spread out of Arabia. Syria was among the first countries to come under its sway; by 635, Muslim armies had conquered Damascus.

The mosque is the center of religious life for Muslims.

Koran school. Religious leaders guide followers, but have no special authority.

Islam imposes an ethical code encouraging generosity, fairness, honesty, respect for the elderly and those in authority, and forbidding adultery, gambling, usury, and the consumption of pork, blood, and alcohol.

ISLAM

Today the vast majority of Syrians are Muslim. Most of these are Sunni Muslims while the rest are Shias, Druzes, Alawites, and Ismailis. "Islam" means "submission to Allah." Muslims consider their religion to be a continuation of Judaism and Christianity, with Mohammed as the last of the prophets and the Koran (also called "The Book") superseding all other revelations from God. In the Koran, Muslims, Jews, and Christians are all referred to as "children of the Book."

Muslims believe that Jesus Christ was a prophet and that his teachings are not "superseded" by the Koran. They think it is blasphemous to believe that God, an all-encompassing spirit, could have a human son. Instead, they believe that Christ's claim to being the son of God is figurative.

Unlike Christianity, where virtually all sects and varieties have an official leader, the followers of Islam do not have a hierarchy of authority. Each mosque has its holy man—called a sheikh—who holds his position as spiritual guide by virtue of his study of Islam and his perceived piety.

THE FIVE PILLARS OF ISLAM

The Koran and the teachings and life of the Prophet guide every aspect of Muslim life. Everything from government to commerce to life's daily rituals and details are covered. The most prominent religious principles, called the Five Pillars of Islam, are as follows:

1. *Shahada* (sha-HAA-da): the declaration that there is only one God and that Mohammed was his last prophet.

2. *Salat* (sa-LAAT): prayer five times daily—at sunrise, midday, afternoon, sunset, and evening. The supplicant must face Mecca, and women must cover their hair and entire bodies (except the face, in some sects). (The picture below shows a group of Muslims praying.)

Throughout the Muslim world, chanted calls to prayer are broadcast from all mosques and become part of the rhythm of life. Before electricity, a *muezzin* would mount the steps of the minarets (mosque towers) and issue the call. Now the calls to prayer are recordings broadcast over loudspeakers. The chanting is still hauntingly beautiful.

3. *Zakat* (za-KAT): an annual tithe of 2.5 percent of earnings above basic necessities. This is used to build and maintain mosques and help the poor.

4. *Sawm* (soom): fasting during Ramadan—the ninth month of the Islamic year.

5. *Hajj* (haaj): the pilgrimage to Mecca, with a stop in Medina to pay respects at the Prophet's grave. This is required once in a lifetime, but only if the person has the financial means to do so.

ISLAMIC SECTS AND OTHER GROUPS

Syria's largest religious minority are the Alawis, who number about 1.4 million. They live mainly along the coast in Latakia Province, where they constitute over 60 percent of the rural population. The Alawis are descendants of people who lived in this region since the time of Alexander the Great. They were gradually influenced by Islam and Christianity. Although they claim to be Muslims, conservative Sunnis do not always recognize them as such. Like Christians, the Alawis celebrate Christmas, Easter, and Epiphany and use sacramental wine in some ceremonies.

A group of Druze men. The Druze originally came from Lebanon; some remained there and others migrated to Syria.

SUNNI AND SHIA

The bulk of Syrians belong to the Sunni sect, with a small number of Shia Muslims. These two sects are the result of a schism in Islam that occurred in the seventh century. After the death of Ali, the Prophet's son-in-law and fourth successor, or caliph, there was a disagreement over who should succeed him. Muawiyah, the governor of Syria, proclaimed himself caliph, beginning the line of Omayyad caliphs, who ruled from Damascus. The Shiat Ali, or followers of Ali, refused to recognize his legitimacy and established a dissident sect that became known as the Shia. They believe that the caliph must be descended from the Prophet. The major faction of Islam, the Sunni, believe that the caliph should be elected. This amounts to a division between partisans of leadership by consensus and partisans of divine right.

Today the Sunni sect includes the majority of Muslims around the world. The Shia sect is centered in Iran and Iraq, where Ali moved his capital. Syria, the homeland of the Omayyad caliphs, is overwhelmingly Sunni.

Because many of the tenets of the faith are secret, Alawis have refused to discuss their faith with outsiders. Only a few of their number learn the religion after a lengthy initiation. Only the men take part in worship.

The Alawis formerly were the poorest of the religious groups, and for this reason they tended to join the armed forces in large numbers. They are now the largest group in the military. Since Hafez Al Asad took power in 1971, the military has been favored and this has caused much resentment among other Syrians.

The Druze community constitutes 3 percent of the population and forms the majority in the Jabal al Arab (formerly Jabal ed Druze), a mountainous region in southwestern Syria. The Druze religion is a 10th-century offshoot of Islam, but Muslims view the Druze as heretical. The Druze have always kept their doctrine and rituals a secret to avoid persecution. Only those who demonstrate great piety and devotion are initiated into its mysteries. The initiated are a very small minority but may include women. Although women are veiled in public, they are permitted to participate in the councils of elders.

The Ismailis are an offshoot of Shia Islam, the result of a disagreement over the seventh imam. There are around 200,000 Ismailis in Syria. Originally settled in Latakia Province, they now live mostly south of Salamiyah on land granted to their community by a sultan of the Ottoman Empire.

SAINT PAUL IN DAMASCUS

The best-known Christian to live in Syria was Saint Paul, one of the main authors of the New Testament. It was on the road from Palestine to Damascus that he was converted from Judaism to Christianity, and he lived in Damascus for nearly two decades. He preached in the Jewish synagogues of Syria for several years. When some Jews plotted to kill him, he escaped by being lowered from a house built on the wall of the ancient city of Damascus. Part of this wall is still standing. Also, a main street in the old city is still called by the same name as in Paul's time—The Street Called Straight—and it is the only straight street that travels all the way through the old city.

Orthodox priests. The 19th-century election of an Arab patriarch of Damascus to replace the Greek patriarch in Constantinople has been described as "the first real victory for Arab nationalism."

CHRISTIANS

The major Christian sects in the country are Syrian Orthodox, Greek Orthodox, and Armenian Orthodox. There are also quite a few Roman Catholics and a handful of Protestants and Russian Orthodox Christians. The Syrian Orthodox Church still celebrates Mass in Aramaic, the ancient language of Christ. Christians account for about 10 percent of the religious population. Christmas and both Easters—Western and Orthodox—are official government holidays.

Most Syrian Christians live in or near the coastal mountains. A drive through the mountains reveals many villages with a church or two but no mosques. These mountains also contain numerous monasteries and convents, some very old as well as some new. Christians are usually city dwellers; many live near Damascus, Aleppo, Hama, and Latakia. They tend to be well–educated and relatively affluent, working more often in the professions.

With the exception of the Armenians and Assyrians, most Christians are Arabs, sharing the same Arabic traditions with their Muslim counterparts.

CAVE PEOPLE

At the beginning of Christianity, most of what is now Syria was part of the Roman Empire. The Romans were tolerant of the religions of the people they conquered, as long as those people did not threaten the empire and at least gave occasional sacrifices to Roman gods. Much later, Christian belief was outlawed and made a capital offense.

Christians were secretive and aloof, would not serve the empire in any way, and engaged in practices that made nonbelievers suspicious. This led to increasing persecution during the second and third centuries. Thousands of Christian believers escaped to the eastern side of the coastal mountains and lived in caves to hide from their persecutors. Just outside Damascus, there are many cave houses carved into hillsides, sometimes high up where they can only be reached by ladder.

The largest concentration of caves is in Maalula, north of Damascus and close to the modern border of Lebanon. Hundreds of cave houses were carved into the limestone cliffs here, and its inhabitants even buried their dead in a cave cemetery.

In the modern village of Maalula, houses have been built over some of the caves and have incorporated them into the living space.

Although there are a few dozen synagogues, most Syrian Jews have emigrated in the last few years. Only a few hundred remain, but they too can observe their own religious practises.

LANGUAGE

ARABIC IS A SEMITIC LANGUAGE along with Hebrew, Aramaic, Syriac, and other ancient tongues of the Middle East. Arabs have a rich oral tradition and, according to some Arab scholars, the oral mastery of even illiterate desert and village Arabs is extraordinary. The use of language is the supreme Arab art form.

The differences between Arabic and English are so great that native speakers of one who become fluent in the other often continue to have trouble with the very different rhetorical styles. These differing styles form the cultural gulf and the different views of life that divide Arabic- and English-speaking peoples.

HISTORY

Arabic is ancient. Its roots go back thousands of years and, because of its holy status in the Koran, it has probably changed less over the last thousand years than any other major language. Arab traders spread Arabic into Africa and India hundreds of years ago, and languages of both those areas bear some similarities to Arabic. Somali and Swahili in particular contain a lot of Arabic-based words.

A fair number of English words originated in Arabic. Some examples include: "alcohol", "algebra", "check", "checkmate", "lute", "magazine", "mosaic", "safari", "Sahara", "sheriff", "shish kabob", and "tariff". The numerals used in Europe and North America were also originally Arabic. Syrians, however, now use numerals that came to them from India.

Above: **Journals are published by government ministries and other official bodies or by religious or professional groups.**

Opposite: **A road sign in English and Arabic.**

Schoolgirls engage in a quiet conversation.

DIFFERENCES IN USAGE

Native English speakers have developed the linguistic and cultural values of understatement, precision, use of logic, and brevity. In other words, say what you mean clearly, and no more. Native Arabic speakers, on the other hand, have developed the cultural and linguistic values of emotional appeal, overstatement or exaggeration, repetition, and words in lieu of action.

EMOTIONAL APPEAL Some Arabist scholars (scholars who study Arab culture) have claimed that Arabs are swayed more by words than by ideas, more by ideas than by facts. Educated native English speakers might be impressed and their thinking influenced by a logical argument loaded with facts and figures; an Arab—either educated or illiterate—will most often be impressed and won over by powerful emotional arguments.

This difference can create a communication barrier. Some Arabs may feel that the cool, detached, fact-filled arguments of a Westerner lack emotional appeal. In a way, it reflects the use of English as a "business and technical" language. However, there are exceptions to the way Arabic is used. For example, newspapers and scientific journals would use more "precise" Arabic, whereas traditional poetry and literature use a more flowery form of the language.

A grand gesture while bargaining at the market.

OVERSTATEMENT AND REPETITION Writing style also varies greatly between English and Arabic. Compared to typical precise English, Arabic is flowery, wordy, and repetitive. Arabic writing often says the same thing over and over in slightly different ways.

Overstatement is also used for politeness. If you say *marhaba* (MAR-ha-ba) or *ahlan* (ah-LAWN), meaning hello, to a Syrian, the answer will usually be *marhabtain* (mar-hab-TAIN) or *ahlain* (ah-LAIN), meaning two hellos, or *ahlan wa sahlan* (ah-LAWN-wa-sah-LAWN), meaning hello and welcome. In other words, the response outdoes the initial greeting.

WORDS INSTEAD OF ACTION Another characteristic of Arabic that is foreign to most native English speakers is the use of threats without action. If Syrians make a threat, they are unlikely to carry out the action. However, people from a culture where idle threats are not often made perceive the threat as real and act accordingly.

The converse of this trait is when Arab enemies (perceived or real) say nothing, that is the time to worry. In Arab villages and among nomadic tribes, "honor" and vengeance killings, though now illegal, often take place with no warning at all when a family feels it has been dishonored.

Arabic is spoken by more than 100 million people.

A man reads notices in Arabic. All speakers of Arabic, Persian, and a few other languages use the same alphabet.

ARABIC DIALECTS

Spoken Arabic dialects are far more diverse than English dialects worldwide; so much so, in fact, that a Damascene has trouble understanding an Egyptian, and an Omani and a Moroccan can understand very little of each other's speech.

The differences in dialects are not only in pronunciation and intonation, but in the use of different words. A Syrian shopping for vegetables in Morocco would find that familiar produce has a different name; the Moroccan would not understand the Syrian words for the vegetables. The Egyptian dialect is well known for using a lot of words that are different from other dialects.

Even from city to city, there are noticeable variations; and the farther apart the cities are, the greater the difference. The dialect in Deir ez-Zor (on the Euphrates River) is quite different from that in Damascus, a little more than 300 miles away.

SOME ARAB PROVERBS

- One who has no good for his family has no good for any other.
- Marriage is fate and destiny. (Meaning: It is not necessary to marry the one you love.)
- Halime returned to her old habit. (Meaning: Human beings can't change themselves, and if they try they will fail.)
- Throughout its lifetime, the tree never reached its God. (Meaning: Don't be too ambitious; be content with what God has provided you.)
- What has been written on the forehead, the eye will see. (Meaning: What has been ordained by God will happen sooner or later.)
- Whoever marries my mother will be my stepfather. (Meaning: I will obey and respect anyone who has higher status or is more powerful.)
- A narrow place can contain a thousand friends. (Meaning: When people love each other, they can fit into a tight place.)
- Feed the mouth, the eye will be shy. (Meaning: If you "tip" someone, he will not hinder your business.)
- Where there are no people, there is Hell.

WRITTEN ARABIC

The Arabic used today for most kinds of writing and certain types of formal speaking is classical Arabic, which is the language of the Koran. Classical Arabic is the same for all speakers of Arabic regardless of region. With the increase in literacy in the Arab world, classical Arabic is becoming more widely known, and some Arab thinkers and leaders hope that eventually it will replace local dialects.

A Koran bookshop. The Koran is the standard for classical Arabic.

Arabic is written and read from right to left. There are no capital letters, but many letters change form depending on their position in a word. In addition, there are several different styles of writing that use different shapes for some letters.

The ancient style of written Arabic is extremely elaborate and decorative and difficult to read, even for most Arabs. The style used in newspapers and magazines, called modern standard Arabic, is easier to read except for someone learning the language. The reason is that the marks indicating short vowels (there are both short and long vowels) and double consonants (there are both single and double consonants) are not used in modern writing. Without these symbols, it is often difficult to know what word a person is reading. Imagine, for example, reading English with all short vowels omitted: "pen," "pin," "pan," and "pun" would all be spelled "pn!"

THAT'S A MOUTHFUL!

There are several Arabic sounds that have no equivalent in the English alphabet. They are as follows, showing the English letter or letters usually used in transliteration (writing a language with the alphabet of a different one):

H (*Ha*): a heavy *h* sound.

kh (*kha*): similar to the *ch* sound in German Bach; the back of the tongue against the rear roof of the mouth does not completely block off the air flow.

S (*sahd*): a loose-tongued *s*; the tip of the tongue is not against the ridge behind the upper front teeth, but the front part of the tongue is flat against the front of the palate; somewhere between *sh* and *s* in English.

D (*dahd*): a loose-tongued *d*, same instructions as for *sahd*.

T (*taa*): a loose-tongued *t*; same as above.

Z (*zaa*): a loose-tongued *z*; same as above.

9 (*ayn*): a vowel formed with a narrowing of the throat; a lot of difference in intensity of this sound between some dialects.

gh (*ghayn*): like a *g* without the back of the tongue actually touching the roof of the mouth; sometimes sounds like *l* or *r*.

' (*hamze*): a glottal (voice box) stop; like someone in the Cockney dialect would say bottle (*bo'le*); the way most western Americans say *t* when immediately followed by *n*: important, *impor'ant;* button, *bu'n.*

q (*qaa*): a stop like a *k*, but made in the throat; Syrian dialect substitutes *hamze* for this.

Arabic street signs. The Arabic alphabet developed from a form of Aramaic. The oldest record in Arabic dates from the fifth century B.C.

Two men talking in a park. Syrians tend to sit close together when talking.

BODY LANGUAGE

When Syrians talk to each other, they stand close together and use lots of hand gestures. They tend to speak loudly as well. Such things are likely to make a newcomer think a fight is about to start, but this is not the case. Even what in the West would be considered an aggressive stance—standing close to and leaning toward another person—is normal in Syria.

There are some head movements that Syrians use to communicate. A quick upward movement of the head with raised eyebrows, often accompanied by closed eyes and a click of the tongue, means "no." A downward nod to one side means "yes." Shaking the head from side to side (like a North American saying "no"), often accompanied by a puzzled look, means "I don't understand," or "I didn't hear you."

Hand gestures here are similar to those in Greece and Italy. Holding the palm turned up with fingertips together forming a tent over the palm while pumping the hand and forearm means, "Wait a minute." Holding the arms out to the side and raised as if to catch raindrops with the palms up and open means, "What's going on here?" Drawing the open hands up quickly above the shoulders, palms facing the other person, means, "That's my point," or "That's my excuse." Brushing the open palms together quickly as if to brush off dirt signifies, "I'm finished with it (or with you)."

Another common gesture is patting the right hand over the heart when meeting someone. This shows affection for the person.

OTHER LANGUAGES

The most popular and widely spoken foreign language in Syria is English, with French a close second. After English and French is German, then Russian. Most educated people speak at least a little of one of these—students in high school are required to study a couple of years of either English or French. Most Syrians who speak another language live in Damascus. Rural areas and villages, particularly in eastern Syria, have few people who speak anything but their own Arabic dialect.

Some ancient languages are still alive in Syria. In Maalula and the surrounding area (an hour's drive north of Damascus), Aramaic—the language Christ spoke—is still used. In the far northwestern corner of the country, the Armenian language is so common that signs are in both Arabic and Armenian. There are a few speakers of Syriac (one of the original languages of Syria) and Kurdish in the northeastern part of the country. Some people in the north speak Turkish, and many Jews can speak or at least read Hebrew.

A sign in English as well as Arabic welcomes visitors to this candy store. Because of foreign influences, Syrians speak a number of languages.

The earliest records of Aramaic go back to 800 B.C. in northern Syria. It is now spoken only in small enclaves in Syria.

ARTS

ART IN MODERN SYRIA mostly takes the forms of language, music, and handicrafts such as fabrics and jewelry. The designs, materials, and even colors are most often determined by tradition rather than imagination.

EARLY ART

Syria's museums contain sculptures and ceramic art spanning many thousands of years. Most of the ancient art was related to function—things such as storage jars, bowls, vases, fighting shields, and images of fertility goddesses. The majority of art in these museums is Roman sculpture and remnants of mosaic floors. The Roman art here is Byzantine (eastern Roman empire) and differs noticeably from that of the western Roman empire (Europe).

Sumerian and Babylonian proverbs reveal sharp insights:

"Who possesses much silver may be happy; who possesses much barley may be glad; but he who has nothing at all may sleep."

"Writing is the mother of eloquence and the father of artists."

"In a city that has no watch-dogs, the fox is the overseer."

Left: **An Assyrian bas-relief from the Aleppo Museum.**

Opposite: **An artist pains-takingly paints an intricate design on wood.**

LITERATURE

Syria has inherited a rich tradition of Arabic literature, in which poetry is a particularly important form. Public recital of odes was a common feature of Bedouin life, and the public reading of poetry continues to be part of Arab life.

Adunis has had an especially wide influence. He was born Ali Ahmad Said in 1930. He was influenced in his early days by the ideal of Syrian nationalism. At about this time, he took his pen name, Adunis, which was the name of the mythical god of Syria who died in winter and was resurrected in the spring. As a student at Damascus University, he questioned both literary conventions and the social and political structure of Syria. He was imprisoned and then exiled to Beirut in 1956, where he has remained since.

Adunis maintains that only radical change in all aspects of life will bring the Arabs into the 20th century. He uses poetry as a means of inducing revolutionary change to create a new society. In his search for revolutionary poetry, Adunis has developed a language that is allusive, evocative, and mystical—and often difficult to understand.

In order to escape government censorship, many Syrian writers have moved to Beirut, which has become the publishing center for the Arab world. These writers see themselves as representing the entire Arab world rather than just Syria.

NEW NOAH

In *New Noah*, Adunis sees the poet as a second Noah, searching for a new life and a new god:

> Our appointment is death
> Our shores a despair we are used to
> A frozen sea of iron water we are content with
> We cross it moving to its end
> We move across and do not listen to that God
> We long for another new lord

One of the most popular of contemporary Arab women writers is Ghada al-Samman, who was born in a Syrian village in 1942. She studied English literature in Damascus and London and then moved to Beirut. She went on to work as a journalist, poet, and novelist. Samman shares the preoccupations of many male writers—identity and loss of self, hatred of the harsh and unsettling social and economic conditions of the time, and the tension between tradition and modernity—but she also writes of the alienation she feels because of her femininity and her intellect.

In *Gypsy Without a Haven*, a woman speaks to her lover who is apart from her. He is married and she is engaged to be married to a man her family approves of. Unable to decide whether to conform to tradition or to break away, she longs to lose her identity for her lover, but also longs to conform: "Two men are struggling for her. One wants to give her a home. Her mask loves the home and she wears it in order to bring a smile to the faces of those she loves. . . , The other man only has for her a new tale of wandering. And she is content with that because a home is accidental and exile and sadness are the reality of human existence now."

> "Contemporary Arab writers have been preoccupied with themes of struggle, revolution, liberation, emancipation, rebellion, alienation. A writer could not be a part of Arab society and not concern himself with change."
>
> —Halim Barakat, Syrian writer and sociologist

ABU'T-TAYYIB AL-MUTANABBI (MUTANABBI)

Mutanabbi is considered to be the last great classical Arab poet. Of Kufan origin, he did his apprenticeship with a Syrian master. He died in 965. No one else contributed so much to the common stock of quotations in Arabic letters:

> Honor the man of noble soul, he becomes your slave.
> But the mean-souled man when honored grows insolent.
>
> Whoso desires the ocean makes light of streams.
>
> Naught will suffice for the understanding of men
> When the light of day itself stands in need of proof.

The *oud*, an ancient stringed instrument that is the ancestor of the European lute, is popular in Syria.

MUSIC

Arab people respond in a similar manner to both language and music, and there are many similarities between the two. The language is repetitive and exaggerated, and so is the music; the language is rich in subtleties, and so is the music; and the language is rich in storytelling tradition about honor, family, and love, and so is the music.

Arabic music is unlike any other, and is dramatically different from western music. Western music uses half and whole notes and often makes great jumps in the music scale; Arabic music uses a lot of quarter notes and makes very small jumps on the scale. The music sounds somewhat baroque—highly decorative—like the music of Bach, although without as much variation on the music scale.

There are two types of native music in Syria. Classical music uses the *oud*, the flute, and small, lap-held drums, sometimes without a lot of vocal accompaniment. Modern music uses an orchestra of mostly European instruments with one lead vocalist and a back-up chorus.

Arabic music has had a heavy influence on other music around the Mediterranean, Africa, and in southern Asia—areas that were part of the Arab empire during the eighth to the 10th centuries. Indian music, for example, has a similar texture, rich in quarter notes, and Spanish flamenco music is a direct descendant of classical Arabic music.

ARCHITECTURE

Islamic art finds its greatest expression in its mosques. The Omayyad Mosque is one of the most important buildings in the Muslim world. It was built on sacred ground that was first the site of a temple for Hadad, the Aramaean god of the ancient Syrians 3,000 years ago, and of a pagan temple of Jupiter the Damascene during the Roman era. The temple later became a Byzantine church dedicated to Saint John the Baptist.

In A.D. 705, when Damascus was the capital of the Arab Islamic empire, Omayyad Caliph al-Walid Abdul Malek cleared the site to erect an impressive mosque suited to the grandeur of the Arab state. The mosque has walls lined with marble overlaid with golden vines and a wooden roof inlaid with gold, while from the ceiling hang 600 gold lamps. It is the finest example of Omayyad art, which spread from Damascus throughout the Islamic empire and became a major influence on the Muslim world.

The Citadel of Aleppo is probably the greatest military edifice of the Middle Ages. Much of the present building was built in the 12th century by the Ayyubids. The *souks* (or markets) of Aleppo, which cover 15 miles (24 km), date from the 16th and 17th centuries and are considered to be some of the most beautiful in the Orient. These picturesque old *souks* are specialized markets, such as the jewelry *souk*, spice *souk*, and carpet *souk*.

The Azem Palace was built in 1749 as the residence of one of the Ottoman governors of Damascus, Assaad Pacha El-Azem. It is considered

The Sayyida Zainab mosque in Damascus.

103

to be one of the finest examples of 18th-century Arab architecture. Each room is designed to typical Damascene traditions, including separate quarters for the *haremlek*, the *selamlek*, and the *liwan*.

Since Islam forbids representational art in its mosques, Syrian decoration has concentrated on intricate geometric and floral patterns. The mosaic tile work of the mosques is particularly impressive. Calligraphy, or decorative writing, is also used frequently in Islamic art.

HANDICRAFTS

Many Syrian handicrafts are unique to the country, especially in their designs and details.

JEWELRY Syrian gold and silver work is extravagant. Bedouins have a centuries-old tradition of making elaborate jewelry for women, and this tradition is evident in modern jewelry. Middle- and upper-class Syrian women wear lots of jewelry: huge, sparkling earrings that often look like small chandeliers, large rings, and lots of

A shop selling hubble bubble pipes in a variety of colors.

bracelets, some meticulously filigreed. These are made from gold, brass, or a gold-tone metal; the educated city dwellers are very class conscious and do not wear silver. It is the Bedouin and village women who wear silver, and most antique Bedouin jewelry is made of silver. Bedouin women and some village women also wear jewelry in or on their head covers and veils, in the form of delicate chains and coin-like decorations.

Elaborate silver teaspoons, cocktail forks, trays, and baskets are also made by jewelers.

CARPETS THAT POINT

When Muslims pray, they face and bow toward the birthplace of the Prophet—Mecca, which is in north-western Saudi Arabia. The supplicants always pray on a carpet. The floors of all mosques are covered with carpets, and people who are praying elsewhere use a special prayer carpet. Some of these small rugs,

such as the one shown here, are made completely by hand by Bedouins. Many have arrowhead designs woven into them; when the carpet is laid down for prayer, the arrows are pointed toward Mecca.

Damascus has always been famous for its marquetry. The different elements of the design are not inlaid individually. Instead, a bundle of lengths of various woods cut in the desired shapes are stuck together. Thin slices are then sawn off and placed on the item to be decorated.

OTHER METAL WORK Brass and copper plates, bowls, and pitchers are common and lovely. The copper work is disappearing, though; it is a tradition of the rapidly dwindling Syrian Jewish population. There are also water pipes and large coffee servers (samovars) made from filigreed brass and copper.

WOODWORK Another Syrian specialty is inlaid woodwork. There are two basic types: one uses thin layers of factory-made veneers; the other has the wood, bone, or mother-of-pearl cut and set by hand. The craftspeople who do the latter can be seen in their shops, painstakingly cutting and fitting the tiny pieces.

There is wide variation in the quality and design of woodwork. Some inlays have only different-colored woods, while others contain bone or mother-of-pearl (most of it now artificial). There are boxes of every shape and size, trays, tables, game boards ranging from lap-size to large tabletop models, and even desks made from marquetry.

Some examples of Syrian creativity in glass design.

FABRICS The fabric arts of Syria take the form of clothing, tablecloths, pillowcases, and carpets. Most carpets made here are created by the Bedouins on horizontal, hand-built looms. The large ones are used to cover the floors of their tents, and small ones are used as prayer rugs. Particularly beautiful rugs are hung on the walls.

Traditional garments with a great variety of embroidery, such as dresses, capes, jackets, and various sorts of gowns for both men and women, are still made by Bedouins and villagers. Syria has a thriving clothing industry. The clothes tend to be brightly colored with an amazing profusion of designs—especially men's shirts and women's clothing. Here Syrian creativity seems completely uninhibited.

DAMASCENE STEEL

During the Middle Ages, sword makers in Damascus became famous all over the Middle East, central Asia, and southern Europe for their swords. Through a lengthy and arduous process these weapons were made so sharp they could cut a floating spider web, so hard they could cut through the shaft of a spear, yet so flexible they could be bent 90 degrees and spring back into shape. The secret alloy from which the swords were made was called Damascene steel.

But these were more than weapons: they were works of art. Through a process called Damascening, the handles were incised with elaborate patterns. The cuts were then inlaid with bronze, gold, and silver.

In the 14th century, one of Damascus's many conquerors carried off all the sword makers and put them in his own service, and the art of Damascene steel soon died out. The process of inlaying, however, lives on even today in the elaborate and intricate workmanship of both metal and woodcrafts.

Tablecloths and pillowcases with unique Damascene designs are now embroidered by machine but are still intricate and striking in appearance.

There is a special brocaded fabric known as damask, named for Damascus. Damascus was on the ancient Silk Route between China and India and the West. The original damask, developed hundreds of years ago, was made exclusively from silk interwoven with silver and gold threads. In the 11th century, crusaders brought it back to Europe where it became popular. Some contemporary handmade damask is still made from silk, but many other types of cloth are also used.

What makes the fabric special is not only its elaborate and elegant designs, but the weave, which creates a raised pattern on both sides of the cloth—perhaps the world's first reversible material.

GLASS Yet another Damascus specialty is handblown glass. There are two ancient glass factories that make glass in three different colors: cobalt blue, green, and amber-brown. Each color is produced for a month, another color for another month, on endless rotation.

The objects range from small tea glasses and bowls to large, brightly painted vases, light fixtures, and hubble bubbles (water pipes). In addition, the factories produce bowls, glasses, cups, ashtrays, and decorative pieces in various sizes.

The prayer wall of Omayyad Mosque in Damascus shows the influence of Damascene steel.

LEISURE

SYRIA IS NOT RICH in leisure-time activities and the people do not have much free time anyway (most of them work eight to 10 hours a day, six days a week). Eating and socializing are the main forms of entertainment—and the only ones in rural areas and villages. Syrians love to talk, and they can do it almost endlessly, often with everyone talking at the same time.

ACTIVITIES FOR MEN AND WOMEN

Social activities generally involve either whole families, only men, only women, or women and children. Some public activities are socially unacceptable for women.

Many older men sit around for hours at the all-male tea houses, drinking tea or Turkish coffee, smoking the hubble bubble (water pipe), and either talking or playing Syria's favorite board game—a Turkish variety of backgammon. Even men who are tending shops spend their time doing these things when there are no customers. On Thursday nights (the beginning of the weekend), young men swarm the streets, just hanging out, looking at young women (who are almost always with their families) and talking. If they have cars, they cruise the streets.

Women, on the other hand, are usually on the streets only with their parents, husbands, and children. Most often, though, they are at home working or shopping for their families while the men are on the streets socializing. Their leisure time is mostly limited to chatting with other women or family members.

Opposite: **A Syrian boy and his relatives play traditional musical instruments.**

Below: **Bedouins drinking hot tea. Socializing over a cup of tea or coffee is the main leisure activity for Syrian men.**

Businessmen playing a board game in an Aleppo coffee house.

SOCIALIZING

Lunch and dinner with friends or extended families are often major social events, with restaurants full until after midnight, particularly on Thursday evenings. During the warm months—from about May through October—dining is usually under the stars, since most restaurants are either partially or completely alfresco. Depending on the work people do, either lunch or dinner can be the big meal of the day. Whichever it is, Syrians often spend two or three hours socializing, eating, and drinking tea. Long dinners are especially common in the cities.

On Fridays, many Syrians who own cars drive to nearby mountain resorts where they spend the day doing the same things they do in the city: eating, talking, and strolling the streets. The mass of people and the traffic jams in Bloudan, an expensive resort in the mountains between Damascus and Beirut, are phenomenal on Friday evenings.

When Syrians go out to for strolls in the streets and parks at night—something they do in hordes in nice weather—they wear their best clothing. Even conservative Muslim women often wear fashionable scarves and dresses. Young people parade around for a potential marriage partner. In summer, ice-cream shops are particularly "hot" places, much like the old soda shops in the United States. For those who have money to spend, shopping is a favorite pastime and part of the nighttime socializing.

On warm evenings, city parks are jammed with people. Children play in the playgrounds while adults talk, and a few young couples even get to hide from the prying eyes of parents for awhile and hold hands, hug, and (if they are daring) kiss.

Relaxing in a bath house in the Damascus *souk*.

CHATTING, GOSSIPING, TEASING, AND MORE TALK

The favorite pastime for Syrians is talking. They never seem to tire of it and it fills most of their leisure time. Men sit in coffeehouses and discuss politics over a cup of coffee or tea and a hubble bubble, while women stay at home and chat with family or neighbors. The art of conversation is well developed, and people are respected for their wit and humor.

Men like to engage in a kind of structured teasing, a verbal game of seeing who can come up with the most ingenious way of needling his opponent. An important aspect of the game is inventing an insult that is both clever and eloquently expressed. These verbal displays are rooted in the long tradition of rhetoric in classical Arabic poetry.

MOVIES, CONCERTS, AND GALLERIES

Many city dwellers spend hours every evening watching television. Those who speak other languages like to watch the multi-lingual channel from Damascus, which has nature and science shows, English, French, and Russian movies, cartoons, and comedy shows. Most other local and regional channels broadcast only in Arabic and show Egyptian, Lebanese, and Syrian soap operas that are often quite melodramatic.

Except for an occasional Hollywood drama, cinemas show soapy Egyptian or violent American and Asian movies. These are mostly attended by rowdy young men. A rare exception to this is the international film festival held in Damascus in the autumn of each year, when films from many countries are shown.

The more affluent Syrians own VCRs, and for them watching videos is a source of entertainment that is second only to socializing.

In general, Syrians love music and educated city dwellers particularly like concerts. Concerts in Syria range from classical European and classical Arabic to Western jazz and Indian pop or folk music.

Syria has a National Symphony that performs two concerts annually at a new performance hall outside Damascus, and the hall is usually packed.

A cinema in Damascus showing Egyptian movies.

SPORTS

Syria has a soccer team and a basketball team, both of which play in a Middle-Eastern/African league. However, there are far fewer sports enthusiasts than in the United States and Europe. The games are sparsely attended, and only a few hours a week of television time is dedicated to sports. Not only are they not sports spectators, but few Syrians engage in athletic activities or exercise of any kind.

A few people hunt birds or foxes and gazelles in the desert, but this is more for food than for "sport." Fishing is also rare and done primarily either for food or as a job.

Some Syrians who live near Lake Al Asad use the lake for fishing and recreation. Swimming in the lake on hot days and rowing small rowboats are the main activities.

BATH HOUSES

Hammams (hah-MAM), or bath houses, are remnants of the Ottoman Empire. They are found in the oldest sections of the cities and are common gathering places for middle-aged and older men. As they do in coffee houses, men are likely to smoke their hubble bubbles here, while relaxing and enjoying a good conversation.

In recent years, Syrian women have become involved in sports, participating in various competitions.

113

FESTIVALS

SYRIA DOES NOT HAVE A LOT of celebrations, and most of the holidays are religious. Chief Muslim holidays are Eid al-Fitr at the end of the fasting month of Ramadan, and Eid al-Adha at the end of the hajj, the pilgrimage to Mecca. Christmas and Easter are celebrated by Christians, but there are not many community festivities for these holidays. Christians usually have a quiet family celebration for holidays, although some decorations appear in shops around the Christmas season.

Important anniversaries, which reflect the sense of national identity following independence, are Revolution Day on March 8, the Birth of the Arab League on March 22, the commemoration of French withdrawal on April 17, Martyr's Day on May 6, and the National Day of Mourning on November 29.

Above: **Two small girls share the limelight at an impromptu celebration.**

Opposite: **A festive crowd gathers to celebrate Christmas.**

SYRIAN HOLIDAYS

New Year's Day	January 1
Revolution Day	March 8
Mother's Day	March 21
National Day	April 17
Labor Day	May 1
Martyr's Day	May 6
Liberation War Day	October 6
Christmas Day	December 25

MUSLIM FESTIVALS

All Muslim festivals vary in date from year to year. The Islamic calendar is based on the phases of the moon, and so has only 354 days. This means that the major festivals occur 11 or 12 days earlier each year compared with the calendar used in the United States and Europe. The dates for Eid al-Fitr and Eid al-Adha are determined by the sighting of the new moon and occur at different times in Islamic countries that are distant from each other.

A pastry shop in Aleppo. Special foods are part of the Ramadan celebration.

Alawis celebrate Christmas and Easter as well as Muslim holidays.

RAMADAN Ramadan is the ninth month of the Islamic calendar. During Ramadan, Muslims fast from sunrise until sunset. From the first light of day until the *imam* can no longer distinguish between a white and a black thread in natural light, Muslims refrain from eating or drinking. This can become difficult if Ramadan falls during hot weather, and young children, the elderly, the sick, travelers, soldiers, and women who are menstruating are excused from fasting, although they must make it up later. People often become very tired during the fast, and life generally slows down. Ramadan is a time for Muslims to focus their attention on spiritual matters, and many families put aside time to read the Koran. The act of fasting proves their devotion to Mohammed and Allah. It also builds self-discipline and instills compassion for those less fortunate.

The celebration comes with the evening meal (called *iftar*) that breaks the day's fast. Food is set on the table in vast quantities, and the

116

family is seated and ready to feast on the food as soon as the minarets sound the end of the day's fast. Once the eating starts, no one says anything for awhile, and unlike regular meals, which often drag on for an hour or more, the food is gone in minutes!

Iftar is made special not only by the hunger that builds up during daylight hours, but by special foods, the sheer quantity of food, and the presence of extended family.

EID AL–FITR Eid al–Fitr marks the end of Ramadan, and people gorge themselves on special foods (especially sweets), stay up all night, and spend their time visiting extended families and friends. People traditionally wear new clothes during Eid. It is also customary for children to get money from their uncles. For a poor uncle in a typically large Syrian family, this can be a large burden. Carnival-type rides for kids are set up in large parks, and young people ride horses and go-carts around the parks and set off firecrackers in the streets. Eid is officially only three days, but if those days fall midweek, some shops, schools, and embassies close for the entire week.

EID AL–ADHA Eid al–Adha is celebrated in about the same manner as Eid al-Fitr. It comes at the traditional end of Hajj, the pilgrimage to Mecca, and celebrates the near-sacrifice of Ishmael (who is called Isaac by Christians) by his father Abraham. During Eid al-Adha, almost nothing is open—government or private—the streets are nearly deserted, and this is the only time the cities are relatively peaceful and quiet.

Men feasting together at the end of Ramadan.

Muharram is the Muslim New Year, and marks the day Mohammed and his followers set out for Mecca on their flight from Medina. It is celebrated quietly with the family.

117

Festivities at a wedding.

OTHER CELEBRATIONS

WEDDINGS Reflecting the supreme importance of family in Arab culture, weddings are perhaps the most extravagant events and the biggest celebrations in Syria. Suppose you are in a Syrian city, walking around late one night, and you hear the sounds of a drum, clapping, and chanting male voices. You look around to find its source and see a couple of men leading the chants, white skull caps on their heads, standing on the shoulders of others who are walking in circles. This a traditional Muslim wedding party.

MAKING A PARTY

Life in Syria is quite simple compared to the West, but this does not mean that Syrians do not know how to have fun. The opposite is true, in fact. Nothing seems to make a group of Syrians happier than "making a party," the English expression they often use. All it takes to get them going (especially the younger generation) in almost any place and at almost any time is some music, some sweet treats, and cola—the name they give all carbonated drinks, regardless of flavor. They clap and sing along with music, and it is usually only a few minutes before some of the men get up and start imitating the movements of a belly dancer.

Arab women do not belly dance in front of men, at least not in public, but the men do. And they love it. They laugh hysterically at each other's attempts to "shake their booties" and bounce their breasts. They "make parties" on picnics, in restaurants, and in the city parks. They get so carried away at times that they dance on restaurant tabletops! Everybody talks at once, and they completely lose themselves in the celebration—a spontaneous festival.

When students go by bus on field trips, they start singing and clapping early in the morning and keep it up, off and on, all day.

While the men are performing this ritual in the street, the women are in a nearby restaurant or home dancing (often belly dancing for each other!), singing, and feasting. When the women finish eating, the men eat, and the party lasts most of the night.

Less traditional people with lots of money usually rent the ballroom at a luxury hotel and eat, drink, and dance all night.

FOLK AND MUSIC FESTIVALS Each September, an international festival is held in Busra, at the site of its amazingly well-preserved Roman amphitheater that seats 15,000 people. The festival runs every night for approximately three weeks and has many international folk dance and music groups. There are also occasional folk dance and music festivals in Palmyra, Aleppo, and other cities. However, these performances attract more foreign residents and tourists than Syrians.

Just prior to the Busra festival, there is a regional festival of sports, music, dance—just about everything—at Sports City (a newly-developed stadium complex) north of Latakia on the coast.

There are quite a few government-related holidays. These are marked with parades, military aircraft shows, and Baath Party speeches.

119

FOOD

HOSPITALITY IN THE ARAB WORLD is as old as Abraham. Visitors to Syria are often surprised at the invitations they receive to visit the homes of locals they barely know or to have tea with a shopkeeper or a stranger in a village. This characteristic is not only religious in origin but is ingrained in the Arab code of honor. Honor, in various forms, is critical to Arab people, and to be inhospitable, even to enemies, causes dishonor.

Meals, especially those eaten with friends or visitors, are a major source of social life and entertainment. Tea or coffee and appetizers can last a long time. A meal is likely to last two hours at lunch, three hours or more at dinner.

Muslims traditionally do not use their left hand when eating, since the Koran dictates that the left is to be used for the toilet. It is traditional for the host to insist that the guest eat more until everything on the table is gone.

Syrian cuisine is similar to that of other Middle Eastern countries. Some dishes have become popular in the rest of the world. Hummus, an appetizer made by blending sesame paste and chickpeas, and *tabouleh*, a salad made of bulgur mixed with tomatoes and parsley, are two examples. *Felafels* (patties made of ground chickpeas) have also made their way into Western countries, as well as the flat round breads called pitas. *Baba ganouj*, a mashed eggplant dish, is another export.

For Syrian Muslims, certain food restrictions apply. Islam forbids the consumption of pork or alcohol, and meats must be specially prepared in a *halal* way.

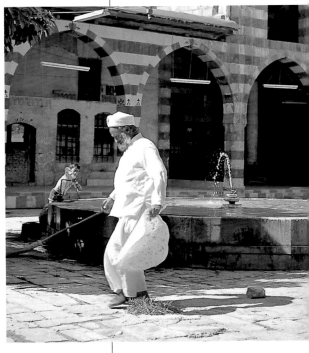

Above: **A man carrying bread in the courtyard of a mosque. Bread usually accompanies meals.**

Opposite: **A dates seller in Palmyra.**

121

INGREDIENTS

Whether served at home or at a restaurant, Syrian food uses essentially the same ingredients: lots of lamb, chicken, dried beans (especially chickpeas), eggplant, rice, and bulgur (cracked wheat). Additionally, olives, yogurt, and Syrian cheese (a white, usually salty cheese most often made from goat's or sheep's milk) are commonly part of meals. There are dozens of varieties of olives, ranging from the enormous to tiny, from yellow to jet black, from bitter and dry to sweet and juicy, and from crunchy to soft. Garlic and olive oil (or purified butterfat) are also used heavily in or on most foods. Coffee or tea follows every meal.

SWEET AND SOUR

Syrians love food that is either intensely sweet or intensely sour. The country has one of the highest per capita consumptions of sugar in the world, and the soft drinks are the sweetest in the world. Even Canada Dry and 7-Up sodas that are bottled under license in Syria are sweeter than in Greece, just a few hundred miles away. Syria's own brands are sweeter yet. The traditional Arab sweets, too, are so sweet a person can only eat one or two small pieces. On the other hand, the pickles are extremely sour, and people generally like to eat sour, unripened fruits and nuts.

Here are some food practices in Syria:

• Most food is eaten by hand or scooped up with bits of flat bread, but french fries are eaten with a fork.

• French fries are the only form of potatoes eaten, and they accompany every restaurant meal.

• All flat bread dips are drizzled with olive oil and garnished with fresh parsley or mint.

DAILY MEALS

For those who eat breakfast, it often comes quite early—school days start at 6 A.M. during the heat of summer, and devout Muslims get up before dawn to pray. Lunch, the largest meal for most people, is around 2 P.M. and is followed by a siesta. Except for special occasions, dinner is usually light and always eaten late; in fact, most restaurants do not open until 8 P.M. and stay open until midnight or later.

Meals range from a light breakfast of olives, cheese, yogurt, and Turkish coffee to special family dinners with dozens of dishes. The main meal consists of a soup (lentil is a favorite), a stew made from chicken or lamb, salads, appetizers of various sorts, different kinds of stuffed pastries, cooked vegetables, bread, and fruit for dessert. It is nearly always accompanied by trays of olives and very sour pickles. A late supper might include olives, cheese, yogurt, bread, and tea.

Syrians make some special foods—a few in large enough batches to last most of a year. One such item is small eggplants stuffed with spiced meat that is then pickled. Small zucchini-type squash are also stuffed with a rice-meat mixture but not pickled. Yet another favorite is artichoke hearts stuffed with spicy meat and pine nuts.

Lamb and lemon stew is a typical main dish.

IN THE KITCHEN

Syrian kitchens in middle- and upper-class homes are similar to, but not as elaborate as, middle-class American kitchens. Few Syrians have such luxuries as dishwashers, food processors, microwaves, and meat grinders. Poorer Syrians—which comprise most of the population—get by with basic utensils and a lot of hard work in the kitchen. For example, garlic is bought in large bunches and first chopped, then crushed in a mortar and pestle. All this work falls to the women of the family, particularly the mother, because few Syrian men know how to cook.

Rural women baking bread in a clay oven.

HUNTING AND GATHERING

Most groceries are bought fresh every day. In modern families, the whole family may share the shopping chores. This is necessary because not many Syrians have cars and the quantity of food needed by a large family is vast.

Shopping for food in Syria is time consuming, because there is a separate shop for each type of food. There are even four different types of bakeries: one bakes only flat bread, a Syrian staple; another bakes baguettes and sandwich rolls; another creates elaborately decorated European-style pastries; and the fourth makes Syrian specialties—dense, rich confections with heavy use of pistachios and sugar water.

In addition to larger shops, there are many streetcorner kiosks that sell candies, toiletries, magazines, and newspapers. In some neighborhoods, fresh local produce can be bought from farmers who trek through with their donkeys or horsedrawn carts, chanting their lists of goods.

Shops in Syria sell a narrow range of goods and are often clustered into special *souks*. One goes to a grocery store for packaged and canned goods, a fruit stand for peaches and apples, a vegetable stand for carrots, one butcher shop for chicken and another for beef, and so on.

125

A street kitchen offers some traditional dishes.

Most dinners end with Turkish coffee or strong tea served in small glasses.

DINING OUT

Syrian food is the same whether it is in Aleppo, Damascus, or Deir-ez-Zor. The only difference is that some dishes vary slightly in texture, flavor, and spiciness. Standard dishes are grilled lamb or chicken; a Syrian specialty called *kibbeh* (KIB-beh), a delicious meat pie made with ground lamb, bulgar, pine nuts, and seasonings; *boorak* (BOO-rok), a cheese-filled pastry; *yalangi* (ya-LAWN-gee), grape leaves stuffed with seasoned rice; various dips made from beans, seeds, yogurt, eggplant, and hot peppers; flatbread to eat the dips with; and various kinds of salads, including *tabouleh*, a Middle Eastern specialty. The menu is the same for breakfast, lunch, and dinner, except for a few things, such as *fool* (fava beans cooked in oil, lemon juice, and garlic, then topped with yogurt) and *fatteh* (a slightly sour concoction similar to hot breakfast cereal), which are eaten for breakfast. There is always a tray of pickles, olives, mint, and raw vegetables—usually radishes and green peppers.

Only a few restaurants serve fish, and it is quite expensive; the Mediterranean off the coast of Syria is not rich in seafood and has no harvest of shellfish.

Only a few restaurants serve alcohol, but carbonated soft drinks are immensely popular, and Syrians drink them with all meals—even breakfast! They call it all cola.

SNACKS

There are no western-style fast food franchises in Syria, but there is fast food. All Syrian cities have small shops that make a sort of Syrian burrito called *shawarma* (SHAH-war-ma). This is thinly-sliced lamb or chicken with garnishes rolled up in a small piece of flatbread. Another type of shop sells *felafel* sandwiches—crumbled *felafel* mixed with yogurt, parsley, and other items and also rolled up in flat bread. Chicken shops sell whole roasted birds stuffed with rice or cracked-wheat mixtures as well as fried chicken.

Starting in early spring, there are decorated carts on streetcorners that sell unripened almonds, a sour treat dipped in salt. After the season for almonds is over, the vendors sell unripened plums that look something like green cherry tomatoes. The cart venders also sell corn on the cob. On hot summer evenings people taking their nightly strolls munch on the corn. A few carts also offer coconuts and roasted chestnuts.

In late summer, streetcorner stands are put up to sell ripe prickly pears, and the stand owner peels them so that the customer can eat the delicious fruit without the stickers.

Finally, there are hundreds of juice shops where fresh juice or juice and milk drinks are made and served by the bottle or glass. Banana milk and strawberry milk are favorites.

A drinks vendor carries a large container filled with coffee or tea for thirsty passers-by.

127

MAZZA

If you have ever had the pleasure of dining out in a real Mediterranean restaurant, you may have encountered the *meze,* or *mazza* in Arabic. This is a huge platter of small tasty snacks that sometimes precedes the main meal but can be a meal in itself. The Syrian *mazza* usually includes flatbreads like pita served with hummus (mashed chickpeas with garlic and oil), *baba ganouj* (eggplant with sesame paste) and *mouhammara* (minced meat with onions and nuts, wrapped in breadcrumbs and oatmeal). *Mazzas* only include savoury foods and, though they are served in small portions, there is a wide variety so that you can quickly fill up. Dining out in Syria in the evening almost always involves a *mazza* before the main meal.

The *mazza* is a pan-Mediterranean custom spanning European countries like Spain with its tapas, Italy with its antipasto, Greece, Turkey, and continuing around the Mediterranean to the Middle East and parts of North Africa. Whether it's the first course or the main meal, *mazzas* are an excellent way to sample the key spices and ingredients of the local cuisine.

Cutting strips of meat in the *souk*.

TRADITIONALISM IN FOODS

The Syrian people, as a rule, are extremely picky about what they eat, and most of them do not even like to try different kinds of food. An exception to this is that many city dwellers (especially teenagers) like pizza, hamburgers, and hot dogs, although these are noticeably different from those in the United States.

As in most other arts, tradition rules in cooking. An example: yogurt is a large part of the diet, used in several different types of dips, as a topping on various dishes, and as a drink mixed with water, salt, and garlic. Syrians even eat plain yogurt by itself. Yet the idea of mixing it with fruit in a blender to make a drink, eating it with fruit or jam mixed in, or using it on a baked potato sounds disgusting to most Syrians. They believe that yogurt should only be eaten the way they have traditionally eaten it.

The Syrians follow the tradition of hospitality shown in the Koran. Have you heard the story of Abraham's honored guests? They went in to him and said, "Peace!"

"Peace!" he answered and, seeing that they were strangers, betook himself to his family and returned with a fatted calf. He set it before them, saying, "Will you not eat?"

TABOULEH (CRACKED WHEAT SALAD)

1 cup cracked wheat (fine)
2 bunches parsley
2 cucumbers
3 tomatoes
2 tablespoons of olive oil
1 tablespoon of salt
juice of one lemon

Wash the wheat and leave it soaking in water for half an hour. Chop up all the vegetables very finely. Drain the wheat and mix in all the vegetables. Add oil, lemon, and salt. Mix well. Let it marinate in the refrigerator a few hours. Serve in a bowl or on a bed of lettuce.

BAKLAWA

1½ pounds chopped walnuts
½ cup sugar
½ teaspoon ground cardamom
1 pound melted sweet (unsalted) butter
2 pounds thin sheet Fillo pastry
1 cup honey

Baklawa is a type of pastry with nut filling and honey glaze. Mix walnuts, sugar, and cardamom together. Set aside. Brush a baking dish measuring about 9x13x2 inches with some of the melted butter. Spread one Fillo sheet flat in the pan, brush with about 1 teaspoon butter. Stack about 15 Fillo sheets using this method. Spread one half of the stuffing mixture on the Fillo sheets. Spread and butter about five Fillo sheets on top of the first layer of stuffing. Spread the remaining half of the stuffing on top. Spread and butter about 15 Fillo sheets to make the top and final layer. Use more butter if you run out, or use less for each Fillo layer. With a sharp knife, cut into diamond, or square shapes. Pour remaining melted butter on top. Bake in a 350 ⁰F (176.7 ⁰C) oven for about 30 minutes, or until the surface turns light golden color. Pour honey over the Baklawa. When at room temperature, transfer individual pieces onto a serving dish. Serve at room temperature or chilled.

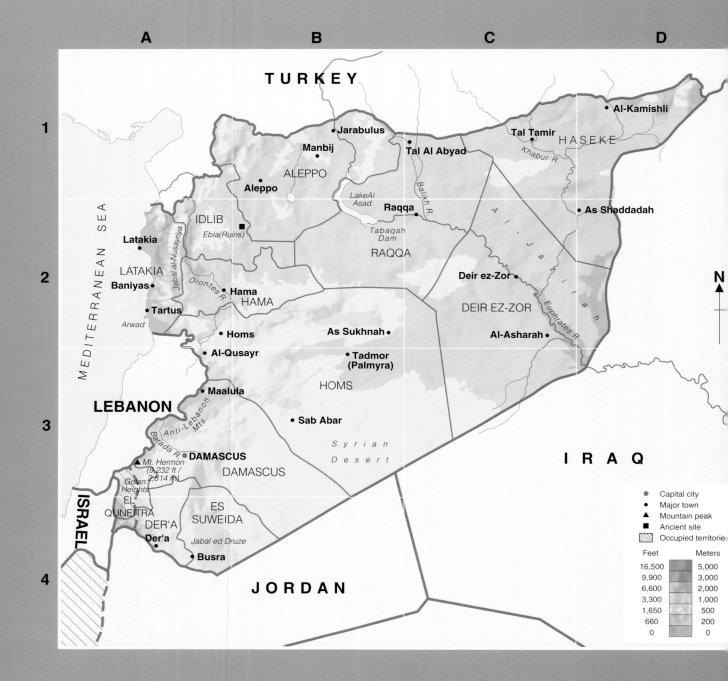

	A	B	C	D

TURKEY

1

MEDITERRANEAN SEA

- Jarabulus
- Manbij
- **ALEPPO**
- **Aleppo**
- Tal Al Abyad
- Tal Tamir
- HASEKE
- Al-Kamishli

Khabur R.

IDLIB

Ebla(Ruins) ■

LakeAl
Asad

- Raqqa

Balikh R.

- As Shaddadah

- **Latakia**

Tabaqah
Dam

RAQQA

A l   J a z i r a h

2

LATAKIA

- **Baniyas**

Orontes R.

- **Hama**

HAMA

- Deir ez-Zor

Euphrates R.

- **Tartus**

Arwad

DEIR EZ-ZOR

- **Homs**

- As Sukhnah

- Al-Asharah

- **Al-Qusayr**

- Tadmor
(Palmyra)

LEBANON

- **Maalula**

Anti-Lebanon Mts.

Jabal al-Nusayriya

HOMS

3

- Sab Abar

Barada R.

S y r i a n
D e s e r t

▲ Mt. Hermon
(9,232 ft /
2,814 m)

- **DAMASCUS**

I R A Q

Golan
Heights

DAMASCUS

ISRAEL

**EL-
QUNEITRA**

**ES
SUWEIDA**

DER'A

Jabal ed Druze

- **Der'a**

- **Busra**

4

JORDAN

- Capital city
- Major town
- ▲ Mountain peak
- ■ Ancient site
- ▨ Occupied territories

Feet		Meters
16,500		5,000
9,900		3,000
6,600		2,000
3,300		1,000
1,650		500
660		200
0		0

N

MAP OF SYRIA

ECONOMIC SYRIA

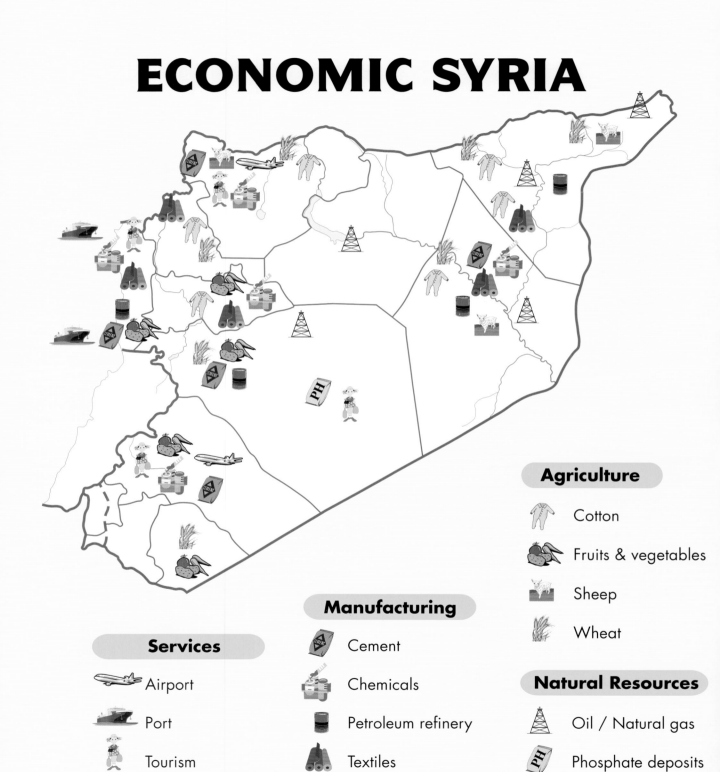

Agriculture

Cotton

Fruits & vegetables

Sheep

Wheat

Manufacturing

Cement

Chemicals

Petroleum refinery

Textiles

Services

Airport

Port

Tourism

Natural Resources

Oil / Natural gas

Phosphate deposits

ABOUT
THE ECONOMY

OVERVIEW
Syria's economy is highly controlled by the government who have implemented modest economic reforms in the last few years, including cutting interest rates, opening private banks, and raising prices on some subsidized foodstuffs. Long–term economic constraints include declining oil production and exports, and pressure on water supplies caused by rapid population growth, industrial expansion, and increased water pollution.

GROSS DOMESTIC PRODUCT
$60.44 billion (2004)
Per capita: $3,400 (2004)

GDP SECTORS
Agriculture 25 percent; industry 31 percent; services 44 percent (2003)

AGRICULTURAL PRODUCTS
Wheat, barley, cotton, lentils, chickpeas, olives, sugar beets; beef, mutton, eggs, poultry, milk

INDUSTRIAL PRODUCTS
Petroleum, textiles, processed food, beverages, tobacco, phosphate rock mining

CURRENCY
1 Syrian pound (SYP) = 100 piastres
USD 1 = SYP 49.24 (February 2004)
Notes: 5, 10, 25, 50, 100, 200, 500, 1000 SYP
Coins: 1, 2, 5, 10, 25 piastres

NATURAL RESOURCES
Petroleum, phosphates, chrome and manganese ores, asphalt, iron ore, rock salt, marble, gypsum, hydropower

MAJOR TRADE PARTNERS
Italy, Turkey, France, Germany, Iraq, Saudi Arabia, Ukraine, China, Russia, the United States (2004)

MAJOR EXPORTS
Crude oil, petroleum products, fruits and vegetables, cotton fiber, clothing, meat and live animals, wheat

MAJOR IMPORTS
Machinery and transportation equipment, electric power machinery, food and livestock, metal and metal products, chemicals and chemical products, plastics, yarn, paper

LABOR FORCE
5.12 million (2004)

LABOR DISTRIBUTION
Agriculture 30 percent, industry 27 percent, services 43 percent (2002)

UNEMPLOYMENT RATE
20 percent (2002)

INFLATION RATE
2.1 percent (2004)

COMMUNICATIONS MEDIA
Telephone: 2,099,300 main operating lines; 400,000 mobile cellular phones (2002)
Internet: 220,000 users (2002)

CULTURAL SYRIA

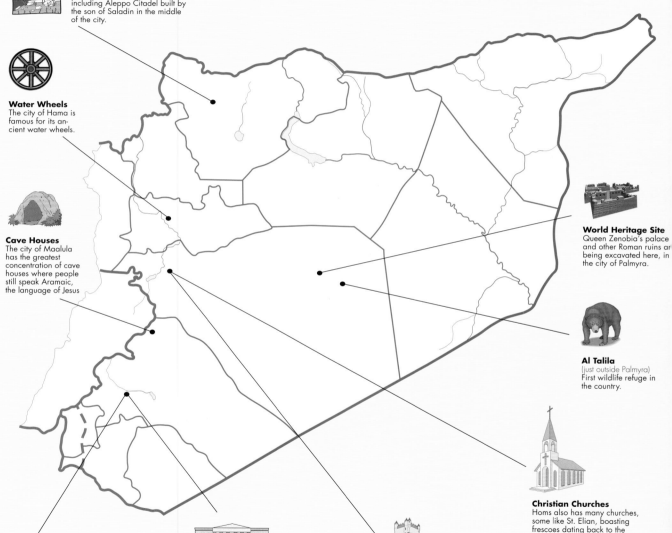

Aleppo Citadel
The city of Aleppo is renowned for Islamic military architecture of the 12th and 13th centuries including Aleppo Citadel built by the son of Saladin in the middle of the city.

Water Wheels
The city of Hama is famous for its ancient water wheels.

Cave Houses
The city of Maalula has the greatest concentration of cave houses where people still speak Aramaic, the language of Jesus

World Heritage Site
Queen Zenobia's palace and other Roman ruins are being excavated here, in the city of Palmyra.

Al Talila
(just outside Palmyra)
First wildlife refuge in the country.

Christian Churches
Homs also has many churches, some like St. Elian, boasting frescoes dating back to the 12th century.

Omayyad Mosque
The famous Omayyad Mosque in Damascus was built 1300 years ago when Islam first spread to Syria.

National Museum
Damascus is home to many museums including the National Museum. It is also the site of some of the oldest *souks* or markets featuring Syrian crafts like Damasc brocades, copper and woodwork.

Krak des Chevaliers
This castle found in the city of Homs was built by the Crusaders and is considered to be one of the most magnificent castles in the world.

ABOUT THE CULTURE

COUNTRY NAME
Conventional long form: Syrian Arab Republic
Conventional short form: Syria

NATIONAL FLAG
Three equal horizontal bands of red (top), white (middle), and black (bottom); two small green five-pointed stars centered in a line in the white band.

NATIONAL ANTHEM
Homat el Diyar (Guardians of the Homeland)

CAPITAL
Damascus

OTHER MAJOR CITIES
Aleppo, Homs, Latakia, Hama, Al-Kamishli, Rakka, Deir-ez-Zor, Tartous

ADMINISTRATIVE REGIONS
14 provinces: Al Hasakah, Al Ladhiqiyah, Al Qunaytirah, Ar Raqqah, As Suwayda', Dar'a, Dayr az Zawr, Dimashq, Halab, Hamah, Hims, Idlib, Rif Dimashq, Tartus

POPULATION
18,448,752 (2005)

LIFE EXPECTANCY AT BIRTH
70.03 years (2005)

INFANT MORTALITY RATE
29.53 deaths/1,000 live births (2005)

ETHNIC GROUPS
Arabs 90.3 percent; Kurds, Armenians, and others 9.7 percent

LITERACY RATE
76.9 percent (2003)

LANGUAGES
Arabic (official); Kurdish, Armenian, Aramaic, Circassian widely understood; French, English somewhat understood

LEADERS IN POLITICS
Queen Zenobia (231–272)
Saladin (1138–1193)
Hafez Al Asad (1938–2000)
Bashar Al Asad (1965–)

LEADERS IN THE ARTS
Adunis, b. Ali Ahmad Said, poet (1930–)
Ghada al-Samman, writer (1942–)
Mutanabbi, b. Abu't-Tayyib Al-Mutanabbi, (915–965)
Ghada Shouaa, Heptathlete and winner of Syria's first Olympic Gold Medal, (1972–)

TIME LINE

IN SYRIA	IN THE WORLD
1200 B.C. The Aramaean kingdom is established in Syria.	**753 B.C.** Rome is founded.
	116–17 B.C. The Roman Empire reaches its greatest extent, under Emperor Trajan (98–17).
64 B.C. Romans, led by Pompey the Great, conquer Syria.	**A.D. 600** Height of Mayan civilization
A.D. 636 Omayyad Arabs conquer Damascus and introduce Islam to Syria.	
1096 French Crusaders occupy parts of Syria.	**1000** The Chinese perfect gunpowder and begin to use it in warfare.
1174 Saladin occupies Syria. His heirs, the Ayyubids, bring stability to the region.	
1516 Ottoman Turks take control of Syria.	**1530** Beginning of trans-Atlantic slave trade organized by the Portuguese in Africa.
	1558–1603 Reign of Elizabeth I of England
	1620 Pilgrims sail the Mayflower to America.
	1776 U.S. Declaration of Independence
	1789–99 The French Revolution
	1861 The U.S. Civil War begins.
1918 Arab troops, supported by British forces, capture Damascus, ending 400 years of Ottoman rule.	**1914** World War I begins.
1920 San Remo international conference places Syria and Lebanon under the French forces.	**1939** World War II begins.

IN SYRIA	IN THE WORLD
1940	
Syria comes under the Axis powers following the fall of France to German forces.	**1945** The United States drops atomic bombs on Hiroshima and Nagasaki.
1946–47	
British and French troops leave Syria, and the Arab Socialist Baath Party is founded.	**1949** The North Atlantic Treaty Organization (NATO) is formed.
	1957 The Russians launch Sputnik.
1958 Syria and Egypt join the United Arab Republic.	
1963 A new Baathist-dominated cabinet is appointed. Amin al-Hafez becomes president.	**1966–69** The Chinese Cultural Revolution
1970–71 Hafez Al Asad is elected president.	
1982–83 Israel invades Lebanon and attacks the Syrian army. After the end of hostilities, Syrian forces remain in Lebanon.	**1980–81** Start of Iran–Iraq War. Israel formally annexes the Golan Heights. **1986** Nuclear power disaster at Chernobyl in Ukraine
1990 Following the Iraqi invasion of Kuwait, Syria joins the U.S.-led coalition against Iraq.	**1991** Break-up of the Soviet Union **1997** Hong Kong is returned to China.
2000 President Asad dies and is succeeded by his son, Bashar.	
2001 Government approves private banks for the first time. Pope John Paul II visits Syria. Syria elected to seat on UN Security Council.	**2001** Terrorists crash planes in New York, Washington, D.C., and Pennsylvania. **2003** War in Iraq
2005 Syria claims it has withdrawn all its military forces from Lebanon.	

GLOSSARY

bakshesh (buk-SHEESH)
A bribe or tip.

Bilad al Sham (bi-LAD ush-SHAM)
Arabic name for Syria.

Eid al-Adha (ah-EED al AD-thah)
Muslim festival at the end of hajj, celebrating Abraham's near-sacrifice of Isaac.

Eid al-Fitr (ah-EED al FIT-ur)
Muslim festival at the end of Ramadan, celebrating the breaking of the fast.

hajj (haaj)
Pilgrimage to Mecca, one of the five pillars of Islam.

iftar
The evening meal that breaks the daily fast during Ramadan.

insha'Allah (in-SHAH-al-LAH)
A common Arabic expression, meaning "God willing."

kafeeyeh (ku-FEE-yea)
A wrapped cotton headdress frequently worn by Syrian men.

Muharram (moo-ha-RAM)
The Muslim New Year, celebrating the departure of Mohammed for Mecca.

Ramadan (RAH-mah-dan)
The ninth month of the Islamic calendar, during which Muslims fast from sunrise to sunset.

salat (sa-LAAT)
Prayer five times daily, one of the five pillars of Islam.

sawm (soom)
Fasting during Ramadan, one of the five pillars of Islam.

shahada (sha-HAA-da)
The declaration that there is only one God and that Mohammed was his last prophet, one of the five pillars of Islam.

sharia (shah-ree-AH)
The Muslim code, a legal system based on the prescriptions of the Koran.

Shia (SHEE-ah)
A Muslim sect believing in the divine right of the caliphs.

souk (sook)
A traditional marketplace.

Sunni (SOON-ee)
A Muslim sect believing in election of the caliphs.

zakat (za-CAT)
An annual tithe of 2.5 percent of earnings above basic necessities, one of the five pillars of Islam.

FURTHER INFORMATION

BOOKS

Davis, Scott C. *The Road from Damascus: A Journey Through Syria* (Bridge Between the Cultures Series). Seattle, WA: Cune Press, 2001.

Gerbino, Virginia Jerro, and Philip M. Kayal. *A Taste of Syria*. New York, NY: Hippocrene Books, 2003.

Skinner, Patricia. *Syria* (Countries of the World). Milwaukee, WI: Gareth Stevens Publishing, 2004.

Stanley, Diane. *Saladin: Noble Prince of Islam*. New York, NY: Harper Collins, 2002.

WEBSITES

BBC News Online. http://news.bbc.co.uk/1/hi/world/middle_east/country_profiles/827580.stm

Central Intelligence Agency World Factbook (select "Syria" from the country list). www.cia.gov/cia/publications/factbook

Embassy of Syria in Washington, D.C., USA. www.syrianembassy.us

Lonely Planet travel information on Syria. www.lonelyplanet.com/worldguide/destinations/middle-east/syria

Syria's Ministry of Tourism. www.syriatourism.org

The World Almanac for young people. www.worldalmanacforkids.com/explore/nations/syria.html

MUSIC

Hamza Shakkur. *Whirling Dirvishes of Damascus*. Le Chant du Monde, 2000.

Hassan Abd Alrahman and Nabil Bouteldja. *Ya Sahi Sabrou: Impressions Of Syria*. Mariposa, 1999.

Sabri Moudallal. *Songs from Aleppo*. Institut du Monde, 2000.

Salatin Al Tarab Orchestra. *Arabian Classics for Belly Dance*. Hollywood Music, 2001.

Zein Al-Jundi. *Traditional Songs from Syria*. Arc Music, 2004.

VIDEOS

Kingdom of Heaven. Directed by Ridley Scott, 2005.

Lost Civilizations, Mesopotamia: Return to Eden. Narrated by Sam Waterston, 1995.

Lost Worlds of the Middle East: Syria, Jordan, Lebanon, Israel. Directed by Rick Ray, 1998.

The Pilot Guide to the Middle East - Syria, Jordan and Lebanon. Narrated by Ian Wright.

The Rough Guide to Cuban Son. World Music Network, 2000.

BIBLIOGRAPHY

Ball, Barbara, M. Brawer, A. Kartin, S. Postavsky, and Z. Stossel, eds. *Atlas of the Middle East*. New York, NY: MacMillan, 1988.

Gumley, Frances. *The Pillars of Islam: An Introduction to the Islamic Faith*. London: BBC Books, 1990.

Lerner Publications. *Syria—In pictures*. Minneapolis, MN: Lerner Publications, 1990.

Pipes, Daniel. *Greater Syria: The History of an Ambition*. New York, NY: Oxford University Press, 1990.

Raintree Publishers. *Civilizations of the Middle East*. Milwaukee, WI: Raintree Publishers, 1989.

Nationmaster Website on Syria. www.nationmaster.com/country/sy

World Gazetteer Online. www.world-gazetteer.com/wg.php?x=1136998929&men=gpro&lng=en&dat=32&geo=-202&srt=npan&col=aohdq

INDEX